ACKNOWLEDGMENTS

The authors and publishers would like to thank the following for their help in the compilation of this book:
The Natural History Museum , London: the Head of Library Services, Rex Banks and his staff, particularly Christine Ellwood and Malcolm Beasley of the Botany Library. The Linnean Society of London: the Council and Librarian, Gina Douglas. The Royal Horticultural Society, London: the Lindley Librarian, Brent Elliott and his staff. Also William T. Stearn, Ray Desmond and Edmund Launert.

They would also like to thank the following for their kind permission to photograph the original prints in their possession:
The Natural History Museum, London, for the plates appearing on pages 11, 13, 15, 17, 19, 21, 33, 35, 39, 41, 43, 45, 59, 61, 67, 69, 71, 73, 75, 83, 85, 95, 97, 101, 105, 109, 111, 113, 115, 117, 119, 121, 123, 125 and 127. The Linnean Society of London for the plates appearing on pages 9, 23, 25, 27, 37, 51, 53, 79, and 81. The Lindley Library, The Royal Horticultural Society for the plates appearing on pages 29, 31, 47, 49, 55, 57, 63, 65, 77, 87, 89, 91, 93, 99, 103 and 107.

Classic Natural History Prints, *Botanical Prints*
First published in Great Britain in 1991
by Collins & Brown Limited
Mercury House
195 Knightsbridge
London SW7 1RE

Created, designed and produced by Studio Editions Limited
Princess House, 50 Eastcastle Street
London W1N 7AP, England.

Copyright © Studio Editions Limited, 1991

A CIP Catalogue record for this book
is available from the British Library

ISBN 1 85585 090 7

Printed and bound in Italy

BOTANICAL PRINTS

EVE ROBSON
AND
NORMAN ROBSON.

COLLINS & BROWN

INTRODUCTION 5

LIST OF PLATES

INTRODUCTION

Campanula persicifolia.
nostras Lob.

Campanula vulgatior
folys vrticæ B.

Io: Iacobus de Rubeis Formis Romæ ad Templum Pacis Cum Priuil. S. Pontif.

Fig. 1

"The art of painting flowers is not a luxury art, and the ornaments that luxury takes from it cannot detract from its unquestionable usefulness. Natural history would be at a loss if deprived of its assistance."

These sentiments were expressed by Pierre-Joseph Redouté, whose prints, particularly those of roses, have made him one of the best loved of all botanical artists. He used his art in the service of science as well as to bring aesthetic pleasure to his public, hoping to captivate the eye of the non-scientific amateur so that he would be guided "from admiration of their portrayal to contemplation of the plants themselves" and thus be added to the numbers of "lovers of botany".

Before the development of printing, no book or drawing could be seen by more than a relatively small number of people. This constraint applied to the earliest plant books – the herbals, originally manuscript books on the uses and identification of medicinal and culinary plants which circulated among the ancient Greeks and Romans. Over the years, continual copying by scribes who knew nothing about plants made many of their illustrations unrecognizable, although they are sometimes very decorative. The invention of printing in the late fifteenth century and the use first of woodcuts and then of metal engravings obviated the need for repeated copying and resulted in the portrayal of plants direct from nature.

The sixteenth-century herbals, with their printed text and woodcut illustrations, achieved a far wider circulation than their hand-produced medieval predecessors. The high point of these woodcut illustrations is exemplified by the herbals of Brunfels (a pioneer work in the portrayal of plants "from life"), Fuchs (Page 9) and Matthioli (Page 11). But only a limited degree of detail

and subtlety can be obtained in a woodcut; and with the advent of engraving on copper towards the end of the sixteenth century, the days of this medium were numbered. The limitations of the medium, rather than any shortcomings of the artist, account for the comparative crudeness of even the best woodcuts. There was no intrinsic lack of technical competence, as can be seen from the exquisite flower paintings in some fifteenth-century Books of Hours and in the work of Albrecht Dürer. Dürer, son of a Nuremberg goldsmith, was one of the first painters known to have painted plants "from nature". His sensitive and accurate watercolours of wild plants have long been admired and have never been surpassed, but only comparatively recently has it been possible to reproduce them satisfactorily. In Dürer's day, at the turn of the fifteenth century, Nuremberg was already famous for its gardens, where "innumerable flowers and foreign plants fill the air with their sweet scents, which the lightest breeze carries into the bedrooms and innermost chambers". A century later, the Nuremberg apothecary Basil Besler published one of the best known early florilegia, *Hortus Eystettensis* (1613), in which the comparatively new technique of copper engraving was used to great effect in portraying flowers growing in the garden of the Prince-Bishop of Eichstatt. In the middle of the eighteenth century, when Dr Trew published his *Plantae selectae* there (1750–1773), Nuremberg was still a centre of botanical activity.

The botanical artist has to combine scientific accuracy with artistic effect, whereas the flower painter may allow aesthetic considerations to take pride of place. The requirement of science that its subject matter be studied at first hand was recognised as early as the thirteenth century, when the Holy Roman Emperor Frederick II, "Stupor Mundi", wrote in his famous book on falconry, *De arte venandi cum avibus* (c. 1248): "Our intention in this book is to set forth those things that are as they are". He urged his scholars to study their material and to take nothing on trust. He had, he said, "discovered by hard-won experience that the deductions of Aristotle, which we followed when they appealed to our reason, are not entirely to be relied upon". His remark has been recognized as signalling a point when Western scholars turned from subservience to tradition towards the methods of modern science. But this early dawning of the age of reason was not to develop into the light of day until long after Frederick's death; it presented too great a threat to the establishments of the time. However, it is this spirit that has inspired generations of botanists in their study of the world's flora. In the field of botanical art, it led to a return to the plant as it grows; hence the significance of the phrase "drawn from nature" or "from life", so often included in the titles of botanical publications.

Science and art combine in varying proportions in the many florilegia produced in France and Holland in the seventeenth century, in some of which plants were drawn very accurately "from life". The term "florilegium", originally meaning "a selection or collection of flowers", has come to designate a work consisting of illustrations of flowers. These florilegia were often collections of hand-painted studies of favourite and rare plants growing in the patron's garden. Sometimes, however, the drawings were engraved and published, thus becoming accessible to a wider public.

Patronage inevitably played a major part in the development of botanical art, for the artist had to satisfy the demands and predilections of his patron and was rarely in a position to indulge in speculative work. In France, the appointment of official court painters established a tradition which helped Paris to become an influential centre of botanical painting. For almost two hundred years from the mid-seventeenth century, a succession of eminent artists held a salaried position, initially that of Royal Miniature Painter, at the *Jardin du Roi*. One of their duties was to add a stipulated number of paintings on vellum annually to the royal collection – the famous *vélins*. Their subjects included both animals and plants, among which were many of the exotic flowers growing in the royal gardens. Famous and influential botanical artists who held the position included Nicolas Robert, Claude Aubriet, Gerard van Spaëndonck and his pupil Pierre-Joseph Redouté. Whereas Redouté is well known for his beautiful colour prints, the best coloured work of the other three artists is to be found in their rarely seen paintings on vellum, which fall outside the scope of this book. However, the small uncoloured engravings by Robert and Aubriet reproduced here provide examples of their expert draughtsmanship and botanical perception.

Robert first became known for his decorative studies of flowers, which brought him to the attention of Gaston d'Orléans, younger brother of Louis XIII, who in 1646 engaged him to make paintings of some of the plants and animals in the garden and menagerie at Blois. These paintings were eventually

Fig.2

bequeathed to Gaston's nephew Louis XIV, and they formed the nucleus of the royal collection of vellums. In 1664, four years after Gaston's death, Robert was appointed Royal Miniature Painter and continued in the gardens at Versailles and in Paris the work he had begun at Blois. While he was working at Blois he had turned his attention to scientific botanical illustration, an interest that may well have been stimulated by the Scottish botanist Robert Morison, who for ten years was Superintendent of the gardens there. So great was Robert's skill that when the newly founded *Académie des Sciences* decided to publish an illustrated history of plants they chose him as principal artist. The resulting publications were landmarks in the history of botanical illustration. The complete work, *Recueil des plantes*, which in its final sumptuous form did not appear until 1788, was never sold to the public and is therefore a great rarity. *Mémoires pour servir à l'histoire des plantes*, containing the first 39 of more

than 300 plates, was published by the Royal Press in 1675. Dionys Dodart remarked in his author's preface that printing in colour was not yet employed and painters wasted much time and were not always successful. All available technical resources were therefore utilised to ensure that the engravings conveyed a wealth of information without the help of colour. Where possible, the plants were shown life-size; but this necessitated the adoption of a large format which, together with the complexity of the engraving, makes the plates rather unsuitable for reduction to a small size. However, Robert's charming and elegant drawing of Campanulas from his *Variae ac multiformes florum species* (1665), one of a collection of delightful small studies of flowers, often complemented by insects, demonstrates his skill as an engraver as well as his fine draughtsmanship (Fig.1). It makes an interesting comparison with Ehret's 18th century engraving of plants and butterflies (Page 29) and Merian's much heavier studies (Pages 15 and 16).

When Joseph Pitton de Tournefort, Professor of Botany at the *Jardin du Roi*, set off on his famous exploration of the Levant in 1700, he took with him the artist Claude Aubriet, who had already made some fine botanical drawings for his *Élémens de botanique* (1694). Aubriet had been working at the *Jardin* as assistant to Jean Joubert, Nicholas Robert's successor as Royal Miniature Painter. His obvious talent had already led to his being promised the royal appointment, to which he eventually succeeded on Joubert's death.

Tournefort, who was well aware of the value of illustrations made in the field, was the first botanist to take an artist on a well documented journey of botanical exploration. "It frets a man" he wrote, "to see fine Objects, and not to be able to take Draughts of them; for without this help of *Drawing*, 'tis impossible any account thereof should be perfectly intelligible." His account of the journey, *Relation d'un Voyage du Levant* (1717), is liberally illustrated with fascinating pictures showing birds, beasts and plants, archaeological remains, Greeks and Turks in local dress, landscapes, maps, views of towns, and even gallows in gruesome detail. It is a remarkable travel book as well as a pioneer work of scientific discovery.

On returning to Paris, Aubriet completed his drawings and engraved many of them for publication. *Symphytum orientale* (Fig.2) was one of the 'rare plants' that he sketched near the gates of Constantinople. With the introduction of engraving on copper, it had become possible to portray the critical, often minute details which the scientific study of plants demands. Aubriet has shown the tiny hairs on the leaves of this *Symphytum* (Comfrey) with an accuracy that could not have been achieved in a woodcut.

Many of the finest botanical artists have been guided by an eminent botanist in the early stages of their career and have thereby gained invaluable knowledge of their subject. Aubriet's association with Tournefort is an early example of such a relationship; other similar associations that influenced artists represented in this book are Ehret's with Trew, Parkinson's with Solander, Franz Bauer's with Jacquin, Ferdinand Bauer's with Jacquin and later with Sibthorp and Robert Brown, Redouté's with l'Héritier and Fitch's with William Hooker.

One of the greatest of these, indeed of all botanical artists, was George Dionysius Ehret, who grew up in Germany and arrived in England in 1736 with a roving commission from the Nuremberg physician and botanist Dr Christoph Jacob Trew. Although Ehret settled in London, his best engraved work, with the exception of *Plantae et papiliones rariores* (Page 29), was published in Nuremberg by Trew, to whom he continued to send drawings from England. Ehret was fortunate in having in Trew a patron who spared no expense in his efforts to see that the prints conveyed the character of the original drawing. Trew's kinsman Johann Beurer, whose friendship with Ehret dated from the days when they were both young men working in Regensberg, supervised the making of some of the prints with great care, and when comparing the engraving of a lily with the original drawing complained that "in its present state it does not look like an Ehret at all". The measure of success that was eventually achieved is evident in *Plantae selectae*, of which Bridson and Wendel wrote: "Although engraved by other hands, its plates still carried the unmistakeable stamp of Ehret's masterly style" (Pages 23, 25 and 27).

Plantae selectae was coloured by hand, a process that inevitably results in some degree of variation. The search for a satisfactory method of colour printing, which offered the possibility of far greater uniformity, was pursued during the eighteenth and nineteenth centuries; but colouring by hand was still used, both on its own and for touching up colour prints. The renowned *Botanical Magazine* continued to publish traditional hand coloured prints until 1948, by which time it had become clear that survival depended upon adopting a more modern and less expensive process. Botanical colour printing could perhaps be said to have reached its apogee in Redouté's *Les Liliacées*. Whether Redouté invented his method or simply developed it to a high degree of excellence is a matter for conjecture; but when he was accused of having appropriated other people's ideas and was taken to court, he defended himself successfully. He explained: "The process which we invented in 1796 for colour printing consists in the employment of these colours *on a single plate* by a method of our own. We have thereby succeeded in giving to our prints all the softness and brilliance of a watercolour, as can be seen in our . . . *Liliacées* and other works" (Pages 79–85).

Although there had been salaried court flower-painters in France since the seventeenth century, no such position existed in Britain until 1788, when Joseph Banks engaged the Austrian artist Francis (Franz) Bauer to draw plants in the Royal Garden at Kew, where new introductions were arriving in ever increasing numbers. It is typical of Banks that he paid Bauer's salary from his own pocket and, by the terms of his will, ensured that it would continue to be paid after his own death.

Francis Bauer came to England to visit his brother Ferdinand, who had returned to Oxford with John Sibthorp the previous year, after their long expedition to Greece, and was working on the illustrations for *Flora Graeca* (Page 71). Continuing botanical exploration, often of remote corners of the world, was reflected in the publication of such Floras – accounts of the plants of a particular geographical area. Expeditions often included at least one botanical artist, who recorded the living appearance of plants collected as specimens by the botanists. On returning home the artist usually had to complete his drawings, and those selected for publication had to be engraved. In the days before the advent of photography and fax machines, print-making offered the best means of disseminating graphic information.

Probably the most famous expedition to include a party of naturalists and artists was Captain James Cook's first circumnavigation of the world, from which Europeans first became acquainted with the plants and animals of New Zealand and Australia. Although the expedition, which was initiated by the Royal Society, had from its inception had a scientific purpose and had included an astronomer, it was only through the foresight and persistence of the young Joseph Banks that his party of "scientific gentlemen" was taken on the voyage. The fact that he personally bore the additional cost no doubt helped, but the Admiralty's acceptance of his party bears witness to a negotiating skill that was frequently to be used in the service of natural history during the next fifty years.

Any excursion into the world of natural history around the turn of the eighteenth century is likely to end up on a path leading to Joseph Banks, who, in the words of Aylmer Bourke Lambert, "dedicated the greatest part of his life to the promotion of natural science and rendering it useful to Mankind". Banks'

hospitable London house in Soho Square was a meeting place for botanists from many countries, to whom the use of its herbarium and library was freely available. Several of the copper plates for prints reproduced in this book were engraved in the "engravers' room" below Banks' herbarium, and his name appears frequently in these pages.

As the number of plant introductions into Europe increased, it became ever more difficult for botanists and artists to keep up to date by producing general, eclectic works, and the monograph became a popular vehicle for publishing collections of prints. Monographs – works dealing with a single group of plants – are here represented by plates from books on such diverse groups as *Pinus*, Heaths, "Geraniums", Foxgloves, "*Liliacées*", Roses, Camellias, Orchids and Rhododendrons.

Authors have produced monographic works for a variety of reasons, which in some cases have been clearly stated. George Brookshaw, in his *Pomona Britannica* (1812), was striking a blow for horticulture in a world which he considered to be obsessed by botany. In his characteristic style, he wrote: "It seems surprising, with all the improvements in the arts, that Horticulture should have been so much neglected, and that Botany should have so generally occupied the minds and attention of men, that they should have been at such immense expense in purchasing the common weeds of other countries, which have no virtue in them, neither have been productive of any general benefit, and at the same time, some of our best fruits have been suffered to be neglected and almost lost for want of attention."

In one of the first major illustrated monographs, *A description of the genus Pinus* (1803–1824), Aylmer Bourke Lambert set out his objects. He sought to promote the growth of "deal timber" in Britain and to bring about improvement of the numerous ornamental plantations around the "Noblemen and Gentlemen's seats in this kingdom", which were composed largely of the Scotch Fir. He attributed this "to the different species not having been properly pointed out, a defect which is here endeavoured to be remedied". He went on to lament that, although new plants were being "sought with avidity in distant regions", little had been done in publishing accounts of the material that had already accumulated in London's museums. His ideas about the reasons for this state of affairs strike a familiar chord today, even though he was writing nearly two hundred years ago, long before the days of television: "One of the causes of this neglect, and perhaps the chief, is the facility of procuring pleasures of all kinds in a gay and rich metropolis, added to the charm of the society in which we live; all these hold out temptations which encroach terribly on literary leisure."

Although the traditional methods of print-making are now not normally used for botanical work, modern techniques of photographic reproduction have ensured that standards of published botanical art are high again, after a gradual decline in the late nineteenth and early twentieth centuries, and the number of very talented botanical artists is increasing. The sheer size of their publications, however, is unlikely to rival that of James Bateman's *The orchidaceae of Mexico and Guatemala* (1837–1843), which poses problems for librarians even today.

Dog Rose

DOG ROSE, *Rosa canina*. Hand coloured woodcut by Veit Rudolf Speckle after a drawing by Albrecht Meyer. Plate 657 from Leonhart Fuchs' *De historia stirpium*, 1542. Size of plate 14¾″ × 9½″.

Fuchs' splendid herbal *De historia stirpium* is generally recognised as the starting point of floristic publication – floristic in this context meaning the study of plants on a geographical basis. Its 519 large woodcuts include about four hundred of native German plants, which represent the first ever attempt to illustrate the flora of a locality. In the opinion of some experts, its publication in 1542 constitutes the high-water mark of the early botanical woodcut tradition, although others would accord this distinction to the 1562 edition of Matthioli's *Commentarii*.

Fuchs was a brilliant physician, and it is clear from his Preface to *De historia stirpium* that he was also an enthusiastic field botanist. He delighted in wandering "over woods, mountains, plains, garlanded and adorned with flowerlets and plants of various sorts", and he realised that "it increases that pleasure and delight not a little if there is added an acquaintance with the virtues and powers of these same plants". The ignorance of his fellow medical men appalled him – it was "almost impossible to find even one in a hundred who had any accurate knowledge of even a few plants". In producing *De historia stirpium* he provided them with an admirable means of remedying some of their deficiencies.

A portrait of Fuchs in his doctor's robes appears at the front of the book, while at the end the two artists and the engraver are shown. Meyer drew the plants "from nature", Fullmaurer transferred the drawings to the block, and Speckle, the leading Strasbourg engraver of the day, did the cutting. Fuchs was concerned that no shading should detract from the clarity of the figures, and he devoted the greatest diligence to ensuring "that every plant should be depicted with its own roots, stalks, leaves, flowers, seed and fruits". This resulted in some delightful, if incongruous, illustrations, such as the one of the Dog Rose bearing two kinds of flowers as well as fruit. The economical use of a single plate to show a plant both flowering and fruiting dates back to the *Codex Vindobonensis* of Dioscorides, which was produced in the early sixth century but which contains plant illustrations that almost certainly draw upon much earlier originals. Fuchs made clear his determination to capture the natural form of the plants, stating that he had "not allowed the craftsmen so to indulge their whims as to cause the drawing not to correspond naturally to the truth". In this he was often very successful, particularly with the smaller herbs; but many of the larger plants have been squeezed into the rectangular shape of the block. The effect can be charming, but it is hardly natural. The rather thin outlines of the drawings and their relative lack of shading indicate that they were intended to be coloured. Colouring was often left to the purchaser, but there is reason to think that some well-finished coloured copies of *De historia stirpium* (including the one from which this plate is taken) were issued by the publisher and that Meyer supervised their completion.

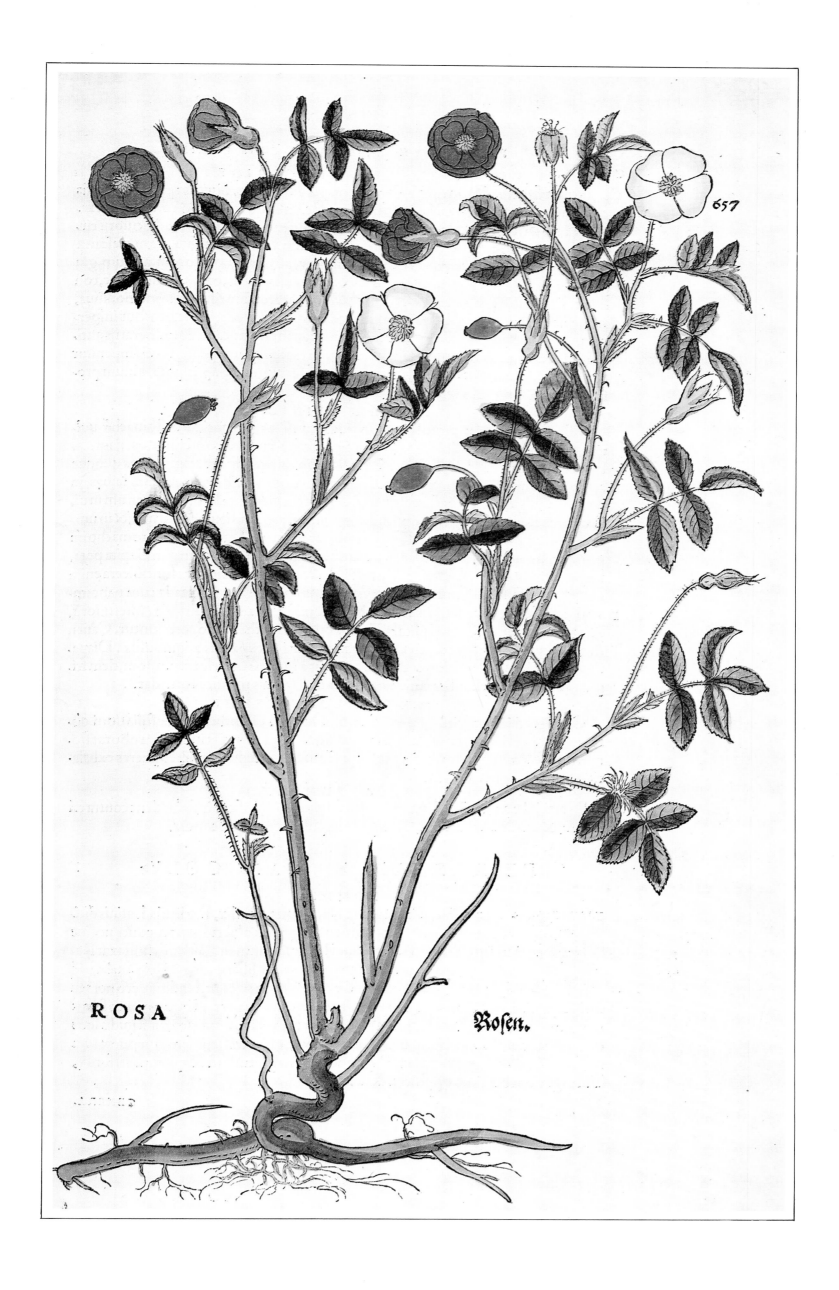

ROSA   Rosen.

657

Squirting Cucumber

SQUIRTING CUCUMBER, *Cucumis sylvestris asininus* (now *Ecballium elaterium*). Hand coloured woodcut by Giorgio Liberale and Wolfgang Meyerpeck. Capitulum 137 of Book 4 (of Dioscorides) from Pierandrea Matthioli's *New Kreuterbuch*, 1563. Size of plate 14″ × 9″.

The Squirting Cucumber earned its place in Matthioli's famous commentary on Dioscorides' *De Materia Medica* by virtue of the medicinal properties of its root, which contains a violent purgative that has been used in the treatment of rheumatism, paralysis, dropsy and shingles. Unlike most members of the Cucumber Family, this species from southern Europe has no tendrils, so it cannot climb; it trails along the ground, and when its swollen hairy fruits are ripe they explode, ejecting their seeds in a squirt of fluid.

Matthioli's *Commentarii* was one of the most influential herbals of the sixteenth century; it was issued at least forty-five times, in various formats and in five different languages. It was first published in Venice, where Matthioli had spent his youth, in 1544, and in the same year the first illustrated edition appeared, in which the commentaries on Dioscorides were complemented by 562 small woodcuts. This edition was reprinted many times, in both Latin and Italian, and some 32,000 copies are reputed to have been sold. Matthioli's fame spread rapidly, and in 1555 he was summoned to Prague by the Emperor Ferdinand I to treat his sick son, the Archduke Maximilian. One of Matthioli's friends was the diplomat Augier Ghislain de Busbecq, who was sent by the Emperor Ferdinand as ambassador to the court of Suleiman the Magnificent. He provided Matthioli with two manuscript copies of the writings of Dioscorides and with living and dried plant specimens and drawings of plants from Turkey. Unfortunately, Matthioli's interest in Dioscorides seems to have become obsessive as he grew older and to have soured his character to such an extent that he ruined the career of more than one scholar who challenged his ideas.

In 1562 Matthioli published a new edition of his *Commentarii*, with completely new large woodcut illustrations and a Czech text; seven further editions followed between 1562 and 1604, with texts in German, Latin, Italian and French. The edition from which this Squirting Cucumber is taken was published in Prague in 1563 under the title *New Kreuterbuch*. It is a German translation of the botanical section of Matthioli's *Commentarii*, omitting the text of Dioscorides, but with the addition of a section on distilling (*mit newen Experimenten Künstlichen Distilleiröfen*) containing drawings of several fascinating stills which no doubt represent the latest technology of the day. Like the earlier small botanical illustrations, the new large ones were executed by Giorgio Liberale of Udine and a German named Wolfgang Meyerpeck, who probably cut the blocks. The adoption of a large size enabled the artists to produce illustrations of generosity and vigour far surpassing those in the earlier edition, where the subjects had to be squeezed into the confines of a much narrower block. These illustrations include some that Matthioli "borrowed" from earlier published sources such as Brunfels and Fuchs. Unlike Fuchs, he ensured that the morphological details of the plants were clearly conveyed by the black line images, which are often strongly shaded, an indication that the work was intended to be issued uncoloured. It is not known when colour was added to the copy from which this plate is taken. Matthioli's illustrations are regarded by some critics as marking the high point of the woodcut, before wood was superseded by metal. Blunt took a different view; he considered them "somewhat commonplace" and wrote that "for all their skilfulness [they] mark the beginning of the decline of wood-engraving".

Von wildem Cucumer.

Cap: CXXXVII.

Wilder Cucumer.   Cucumis fyluestris, afininus.

Gestalt.

 Ilder Cucumer / auch Eselscucumer / vnnd sprin-
gend hundtskürbß genandt. Wirdt von dem zämen Cucumer allein an der frucht vnd
wurtzel vnterschieden / dann die frucht an diesem wilden Cucumer ist vil kleiner / darge-
gen die

Pineapple

PINEAPPLE, *Ananas comosus*. Hand coloured engraving. Plate 57 from Vol. 1 of Jan Commelin's *Horti medici amstelodamensis rariorum . . . plantarum . . . descriptio et icones*, 1697. Size of plate 15½″ × 10¼″.

This stylish Pineapple was growing in the Physic Garden in Amsterdam at a time when most Europeans had probably never seen the plant or its fruit. It could survive in Europe only in a heated greenhouse, or "stove", which made it a luxury beyond the reach of the ordinary citizen. Indeed, pineapples became a symbol of social standing and were used as table decorations at banquets. To our eyes, the pineapple portrayed here may look rather puny, but the artist and engraver have caught their subject's statuesque quality to such effect that it is easy to understand its appeal to architects, who found in it a perfect model for stone finials. The ultimate architectural manifestation must surely be the exquisite little building in the form of a pineapple, built in 1761 at Dunmore in Stirlingshire for the twenty-nine year-old Earl of Dunmore (later Governor of New York and Virginia).

The Pineapple's generic name, *Ananas*, is derived from the Tupi Indian name, *Nana*, while the common English and Spanish names reflect the fruit's resemblance to a giant pine cone. The modern pineapple is a cultigen, domesticated and developed in South America in pre-Columbian times. A mutation for seedlessness occurred, and selections were then made for increased fruit size, juiciness, sweetness and improved flavour. Archaeological evidence suggests that pineapples had reached Tehuacan, in Mexico, by about the beginning of the Christian era.

Europeans first recorded pineapples on the Island of Guadeloupe in 1493, and the following year Michele de Cuneo wrote: "There were some [crops] like artichoke plants, but four times as tall, which gave fruit in the shape of a pine cone, twice as big, which fruit is excellent . . . and it seems to be wholesome." A later traveller considered pineapples "the finest fruit in existence". Sadly, it proved almost impossible to bring the fruit back to Europe in good condition; but after the discovery of the New World by Europeans, the cultivation of pineapples spread rapidly throughout the tropics. Although methods of transport gradually improved, it was the development of the canning industry at the end of the nineteenth century that brought this delicious fruit to the tables of millions of new consumers.

Commelin's book illustrates and describes some of the choice plants growing in the Amsterdam *Hortus Medicus*, or Physic Garden, which he and his fellow senator, Jan Huydercoper (to whom the book is dedicated) had transferred to a new and better site in the city. Commelin had provided many plants for the garden, including exotics from the Orient, where the Dutch East India Company was trading very actively. Newly discovered plants were being brought from the Dutch colonies in the Cape, Malabar and Coromandel, the Indies and Ceylon, and also from the West Indies. *Horti medici amstelodamensis etc.* appeared in two volumes, the first of which, on the plants of the East and West Indies, was Jan Commelin's most important contribution to botanical knowledge. He did not live to see his work completed; that task fell to his nephew, Caspar Commelin. The illustrations were mainly the work of Johan and Maria Monincx. According to Blunt, the engravers took considerable liberties with the drawings and, though the detail is finely executed, they have "not succeeded in giving any idea of the quality of the originals". Nevertheless, the work is one of considerable distinction, heralding a golden age of European engraving.

Cocoa

COCOA, CACAU BOOM, *Theobroma cacao*. Hand coloured engraving by P. Sluyter after a drawing by Maria Sibylla Merian. Plate 26 from her *De metamorphosibus insectorum Surinamensium*, 1705. Size of plate 19″ × 13¼″.

*T*heobroma (Food of the Gods), the generic name that Linnaeus coined for the Cocoa Tree, indicates the high opinion that Europeans had of its products, cocoa and chocolate. This native of lowland tropical America is a small tree with large leaves and, as shown here, flowers and fruits borne directly on the bark of the larger branches. Inside the pod are several seeds about the size of lima beans which, when fermented, dried and roasted, yield chocolate. Cocoa is produced by removing most of the fatty oils, which are then used as cocoa butter.

Cocoa was apparently first cultivated in Mexico, where the Conquistadores found that chocolate was a drink prized by the Aztecs. In seventeenth-century Europe chocolate became a fashionable and expensive "social" drink, and chocolate-houses were favourite gathering places for men of affairs. At first it was a drink for men only; but once the idea of diluting it by the addition of milk was accepted, it was considered suitable for women. Chocolate was believed to be a powerful aphrodisiac, for which it was valued by the Aztecs and even by Casanova. Its nutritious qualities, too, did not escape the notice of Europeans, for such a concentrated form of food had obvious military value.

Maria Sybilla Merian's story is extraordinary. She was a pioneer in the art of entomological illustration, and in her domestic life and foreign travel she exercised an independence which might be considered unorthodox even now, three hundred years later. She was born in Frankfurt into a family of artists. Her Swiss father, Matthaus Merian the Elder, was an engraver of some note, but she can have known little of him as he died when she was about three years old. Her mother, daughter of the artist Johann Theodor de Bry, married as her second husband the Dutch flower painter Jacob Marell. He had many pupils and it is not surprising that, in an environment of artistic activity, Maria's talent developed at an early age. Her partiality for drawing insects was at first discouraged by her mother, but Blunt relates that, on recollecting that she herself had collected "caterpillars, shells and stones" during her pregnancy, she relented and allowed Maria to follow her inclination.

Maria's first publication was a volume of engravings of European insects (1679); this was followed in 1680 by a very different work, *Neues Blumenbuch*, a charming series of hand-painted engravings of garden flowers, based on Nicholas Robert's *Diverses Fleurs* (1660) and intended as models for embroidery. Maria married one of her step-father's pupils, Johann Graff of Nuremberg, and had two daughters; but after many years of married life she joined an extreme Protestant sect, the Labadists, and left her husband. Taking her daughters, she went to live in the Labadist community at the castle of Bosch, in Friesland. Her husband tried to persuade her to return to him; but the Labadists did not regard marriage with outsiders as binding, and his efforts were doomed to failure.

It was Maria's discovery in the castle of Bosch of a collection of gorgeous butterflies from Surinam that was to determine the next chapter in her life's story. Inspired by the butterflies and also, according to Goethe, by the young Charles Plumier, whose botanical exploits in the West Indies were then becoming known in Europe, Maria set sail for Surinam in 1698, taking her younger daughter, Dorothea, who had helped with her work on European insects. They studied and drew the insects and plants of Surinam, which at that time included present-day Guyana; but after two years Maria's poor health forced them to return to Europe.

P. Sluyter Sculp.

Okra

OKRA, LADY'S FINGERS, *Ketmia brasiliensis* etc. (now *Abelmoschus esculentus*).
Hand coloured engraving by P. Sluyter after a drawing by Maria Sibylla
Merian. Plate 37 from her *De metamorphosibus insectorum Surinamensium*,
1705. Size of plate 19″ × 13¼″.

The first impression given by this "*Ketmia*" is of a plant with flowers of
different colours. A tendency to produce this effect, which is a factor of
ageing, is present in various members of the Mallow Family, to which
Abelmoschus belongs. Merian mentioned this phenomenon in the caption to
her drawing; but she was more interested in the little moth that developed
from the caterpillar that was eating the leaves. Of the *Ketmia* she wrote:
"This plant was called in Surinam Okkerum or Althea . . . slaves in America
cook and eat the fruit . . . it has two kinds of blossom, one yellowish–white
and the other pink in colour." Okra, or Lady's Fingers, is one of the popular
tropical vegetables now to be found in food shops in Britain. Its fruits,
which are 4½–6 ins. long, six-sided and finger-like, are gathered while they
are still unripe and tender and are cooked or used in salads. The ripe seeds are
a source of oil for margarine. The leaves are variable; and though those
illustrated by Merian are perhaps not typical, they fall within the range of
variation of the species. They were obviously suffering from the activities of
predatory caterpillars.

Maria Merian may be regarded as first and foremost a scientist; indeed, she
herself considered her artistic achievements as being in the service of science.
Occasionally, however, she fell short of scientific accuracy, as when she
depicted the Cashew Nut attached to its stalk by the wrong end. But botany
was not her first concern; that clearly lay in the field of entomology.
Although plants play their part in her distinctive and well-balance designs, it
is the delicate detail and beauty of the insects, and in particular of the often
dazzling butterflies, that catch the eye. The plants, by contrast, sometimes
look somewhat crude.

De metamorphosibus insectorum Surinamensium was published in Amsterdam
in 1705, with plates engraved mainly by Jan Sluyter and Joseph Mulder; and
a second edition appeared in 1714 with additional plates provided by Maria's
elder daughter, Johanna, who had settled in Surinam. Maria Merian often
shaded in her drawings with a wealth of straight lines, which provided an
easily copied model for her engravers but gives the prints a rather heavy look
that is, however, quite in keeping with the baroque character of her designs.

37

Carolina Allspice

CAROLINA ALLSPICE, *Frutex corni foliis conjugatis* etc. (now *Calycanthus floridus*). Hand coloured engraving by Mark Catesby. Plate 46 from Vol. 1 of his *The natural history of Carolina, Florida and the Bahama Islands*, 1731–1743. Size of plate 20″ × 14″.

In this illustration Catesby has combined his two subjects into a decorative composition which, for all its stylistic differences, is reminiscent of the work of that earlier pioneer of American natural history, Maria Sybilla Merian (Pages 14 and 17). Like Merian, he composed his drawings with an ecological purpose, showing the birds with "those plants on which they fed, or [had] any relation to". Here a chatterer (*Garrulus carolinensis*) sits in the branches of *Calycanthus floridus*, one of the species which Catesby introduced into England. It would seem that this Carolina Allspice, with its aromatic bark – "as odoriferous as cinnamon" – and attractive flowers, was not in cultivation even in America at that time, for Catesby found it "in the remote and hilly parts of Carolina but no where amongst the inhabitants". In choosing which trees and shrubs to illustrate, he gave priority to those which he thought would flourish in the English climate and those with commercial or medical potential, "particularly the forest trees, shrubs and other plants, not hitherto described, or very incorrectly figured by authors".

Several drawings in *The natural history of Carolina* have a distinctly oriental flavour, suggested in part by their two-dimensional quality. Catesby's decision to work in this "flat" manner stemmed from his lack of training in draughtsmanship. He could be said to have made a virtue out of necessity, for he explained: "As I was not bred a Painter I hope some faults in Perspective, and other Niceties, may be more readily excused, for I humbly conceive Plants, and other things done in a Flat, tho' exact manner, may serve the purpose of Natural History better in some measure than in a more bold and Painter like way."

The fact that this pioneer work on the natural history of eastern North America was ever published is testimony to Catesby's industry and tenacity. Although he had studied natural history before going to America, he was not a trained artist and would therefore require the services of an engraver. On returning to London with his records and drawings, his intention has been to seek a publisher in Paris or Amsterdam; but he was advised that, although his work was well worth publishing, the expense of having the plates engraved was likely to be so great that it would be better to abandon the idea. Fortunately he did not let matters rest there. In his own words: "At length by the kind advice and Instructions of that inimitable Painter, Mr Joseph Goupy, I undertook and was initiated in the way of etching them myself, which, tho' I may not have done in a Graver-like manner, choosing rather to omit their method of cross-Hatching, and to follow the humour of the Feathers, which is more laborious, and I hope has proved more to the purpose." He engraved more than two hundred plates and supervised their colouring; it was a remarkable achievement.

T. 46

Frutex Corni folijs &c.

Garrulus Carolinensis.
The Chatterer.

Balsam Tree

BALSAM TREE, PITCH APPLE, *Cenchramidea* (now *Clusia rosea*). Hand coloured engraving by Mark Catesby. Plate 99 from Vol. 2 of his *The natural history of Carolina, Florida and the Bahama Islands*, 1731–1743. Size of plate 20″ × 14″.

The stiff, almost artificial appearance which Catesby has given to this strange plant is not greatly exaggerated, for Clusias do sometimes look rather like wax models. They are unusual among trees and shrubs in that they are epiphytic, growing on other plants or even on bare rocks; but they are not parasites. In their habitats the supply of moisture available to the roots is erratic, and an ability to retain it is vital. Thick leathery leaves are characteristic of plants which manage to survive in such conditions. They often show a superficial and misleading similarity to the thick, fleshy succulents which are adapted to the very different conditions of the desert. Clusias and their close relatives are plants of tropical American rainforests; Catesby's *Clusia rosea*, which he found in the Bahamas, was growing on the extreme northern edge of the distribution of the genus. Each *Clusia* tree bears only one sex of flower; here they are female. The apple-sized fruit splits, releasing many sticky red-coated seeds, which adhere to rocks or, like mistletoe seeds, to branches. This species of *Clusia* yields a resin which was used to cure sores in horses and as a substitute for tallow in boats and other vessels, hence the name Pitch Apple.

Catesby engraved his own plates and personally supervised their colouring. On the subject of colour, in particular his choice of greens, he explained that his principal concern was to use "those most resembling nature, that were durable and would retain their lustre". He was well aware, however, that leaf colour is a transient phenomenon; the artist has to be content with catching a moment in time. "There is", he wrote, "no degree of Green but what some Plants are possessed of at different times of year, and the same Plant changes its colour gradually with its Age." He could not have expressed the problem more clearly. In an effort to portray his plants in as life-like a manner as possible, he always drew them when they were freshly gathered.

Catesby has been called the Father of American ornithology, though he played an important role in the study of American natural history in a much wider field. Plants were his first and greatest interest, but his American book is best known for its zoological content. *The natural history of Carolina* contains descriptions and illustrations of various species of the flora and fauna of the area, including fish, reptiles and, above all, birds. Many of these had not previously been recorded, but the plants of eastern North America were far better known at that time than the animals.

Pawpaw

PAWPAW, *Papaya fructo oblongo* etc. (now *Carica papaya*). Hand coloured engraving by J.J. Haid after a drawing by Georg Dionysius Ehret. Plate 7 from Part 1 of Christoph Jacob Trew's *Plantae selectae*, 1750–1773. Size of plate 19½" × 14".

Plantae selectae, one of the great European botanical iconographies, was published towards the beginning of a hundred-year period which might well be regarded as the golden age of European botanical prints. Its pages bears witness to the coming together of three vital elements: a superb artist, engraving of the very highest quality, and an enlightened and wealthy patron. However, these would have been of little use without the botanical riches that were arriving in Europe as trading and colonisation opened up the world, providing an abundance of material worthy of illustration.

Following his permanent settlement in England in 1736, Ehret found plentiful patronage among British plant collectors and continued to send drawings of exotic plants to his old patron and compatriot Dr Trew in Nuremberg. By 1742 Trew had received over a hundred of these drawings, and he proposed that they should be engraved and published. It was not until 1748, however, that he arranged with the distinguished Nuremberg engraver Johann Jacob Haid to have forty plates engraved annually. The first set of twelve plates (termed a Decuria) of *Plantae selectae* was issued two years later. The Haid family were leading exponents of their art and adapted their own sophisticated manner of etching to produce a strongly modelled image which is particularly appropriate to Ehret's firm and vigorous style.

The Pawpaw may not be best known for its decorative qualities, but as portrayed by Ehret it can certainly hold its own in Trew's collection predominantly of ornamental exotics. This distant relative of the Passion Flower Family is a short-lived tree that has been cultivated in Central America and Brazil since pre-Columbian times. The Spanish found it in Panama and took it to the West Indies, from where it reached Europe, probably in the seventeenth century.

Pawpaw trees normally bear only male or only female flowers; but the female trees sometimes have one or two bisexual flowers, as Ehret has shown in this drawing (a). The large yellowish-green fruits contain a juicy pulp which has a delicate taste similar to that of a musk melon. It is a favourite breakfast fruit in the tropics and contains an enzyme (papain) that is used for tenderising meat.

The first Pawpaw to flower in England grew in one of Lord Petre's stoves (then the largest and most numerous in the country) at Thorndon in Essex, and it was there that Ehret drew it for his *Plantae et papiliones rariores*. It is possible that one of the Thorndon plants provided the model for this pawpaw in *Plantae selectae*, but it might have been growing in several of the interesting gardens which Ehret visited on his travels round England. He spent much of his time making drawings at the Apothecaries' Garden, Chelsea Physic Garden, into which new plants were constantly being introduced. It held other attractions, too, for it was in the care of Philip Miller, whose sister-in-law became Ehret's wife.

Tab. VII.

a. *Flos hermaphroditus*, b. *flos femininus*, c. *fructus rudimentum durissimum*, d. *calyx...*, e. *semen pedicula... radicula ad... ...*

PAPAYA
fructu oblongo
Melonis effigie
Tournef. Infit. r. Reg. Par.
Cat. Species p. 20

P. Par. J. Cuid. exc... Aug. Vind.

Tulip Tree

TULIP TREE, *Liriodendrum foliis angulatis truncatis* etc. (now *Liriodendron tulipifera*). Hand coloured engraving by J.J. Haid after a drawing by Georg Dionysius Ehret. Plate 10 from Part 1 of Christoph Jacob Trew's *Plantae selectae*, 1750–1773. Size of plate 19½″ × 14″.

The unmistakable shape of the leaf of the Tulip Tree does not suggest that it is, in fact, a member of the *Magnolia* Family; but the inner parts of the flower, shown clearly in Ehret's drawing, reveal its true affinity. Like several other natives of eastern North America, it has a close relative in China, a distribution resulting from the last Ice Age. Before then, it grew over a much wider area of the Northern Hemisphere.

The Tulip Tree was one of the earliest introductions into Europe from North America. It had probably been in cultivation for some time in England before Bishop Compton's tree in Fulham Palace garden, in London, was mentioned in 1688. Its tulip-like flowers are less conspicuous than those of *Magnolia*, but the tall striking trunk and unusual leaves help to make it a desirable plant for the large garden or arboretum. The timber is used extensively in North America, mainly for joinery.

Ehret's drawing displays two qualities characteristic of his work: an objective precision that makes the subject appear almost to stand out from the page, and an unerring sense of design. Clarity and design were allied to a scientist's eye for detail, which is shown in the analyses. This scientific awareness stemmed from a crucial event in Ehret's life. When he was working in Regensberg, in his early twenties, Ehret formed a firm friendship with Johann Beurer, an apothecary and botanist, who was related to the eminent Nuremberg physician Christoph Jacob Trew. Through Beurer, Ehret met Trew, who became his life-long friend and patron. Trew, a keen botanist and a wealthy benefactor of natural history, recognised Ehret's talent and, realising that he lacked botanical knowledge, encouraged him to study the structure and form of his subjects. Ehret applied himself to the task to such effect that his drawings acquired an accuracy that has made them valuable to modern botanists as a means of identifying exotic plants named using a different system of nomenclature. He was thus well equipped to do exact botanical work by the time that he met Carl Linnaeus in Holland in 1736. Linnaeus demonstrated his new method of examining the stamens of flowers for the purpose of classification, and Ehret resolved "to bring out a Tabella of it". His table showing the Linnaen Sexual System of classification became famous and was pirated more than once. The system was, for a time, the accepted basis of classification, and several authors were inspired to publish illustrated works expounding it (see Pages 31, 39, 41, 55 and 57).

Ehret made drawings of ornamental plants for patrons in both England and Germany, and in these he often included analyses; his botanical knowledge and accuracy enabled him to produce works of scientific value as well as of great beauty. Later in life he contributed articles to learned journals, and he drew corals as well as plants. Recognition of his scientific achievements was marked by his election to the Royal Society in 1757, and he was also honoured in his native Germany.

Tab. X.

LIRIODENDRVM foliis angulatis truncatis.

Swamp Lily

SWAMP LILY, *Lilium foliis sparsis* etc. (now *Lilium superbum*). Hand coloured engraving by J.J. Haid after a drawing by Georg Dionysius Ehret. Plate 11 from Part 1 of Christoph Jacob Trew's *Plantae selectae*, 1750–1773. Size of plate 19½″ × 14″.

Lilies have long been regarded as very special plants. They were accorded a place in religious iconography at least as long ago as the second millenium BC, when their association with Minoan shrines foreshadowed the adoption by Christians, many centuries later, of *Lilium candidum* as the Madonna Lily. But this species, aptly named *Lilium superbum*, was unknown to Europeans until they discovered the New World.

We have become so accustomed to being surrounded by the botanical riches of the world that it is hard to imagine the impression made by the first sight of plants such as this. It is tempting to speculate upon Ehret's reaction to this charming floriferous lily; something about it inspired him to put aside any idea of producing a comprehensive morphological record, allowing the inflorescence to dominate the page with its candelabrum of scintillating pendant flowers.

The exact date of introduction of *Lilium superbum* into England is unknown, but it was growing before 1727 at Eltham, in Kent, where the prosperous London apothecary James Sherard created a garden famous for its collection of exotic and rare plants. In building up his collection, James was greatly helped by his brother William, an eminent botanist who had encouraged Mark Catesby to return to America and work on *The natural history of Carolina, etc.* (Pages 19 and 21). It is highly likely that the Swamp Lily was one of Catesby's introductions; it is large and very vigorous and is found in the wild from Canada to the Carolinas, in wet meadows and marshy ground.

As trade with eastern North America developed, increasing numbers of plants from the area were introduced into cultivation in Europe. One of the most notable collections was built up by Peter Collinson, a Quaker haberdasher and mercer with business connections in the North American colonies and the West Indies. Collinson's interest in American plants had first been aroused by Catesby, who had introduced a wealth of new species into English gardens. A visiting Swedish naturalist wrote that Collinson's garden at Peckham, then a pretty village about three miles from London, was "full of rare plants, especially those from America", and it was in that garden in 1738 that Ehret found the American Swamp Lily portrayed here. Eight years later Collinson moved to Mill Hill, Middlesex, where he created a renowned botanical garden. According to his friend John Fothergill, Collinson was "the means of introducing more new and beautiful plants into Britain than any man of his time". It was partly due to Collinson's influence that in 1765 John Bartram, a fellow Quaker who had collected many plants for him, was appointed Botanizer Royal for America.

Many of the new plants from America and other parts of the world were drawn by Ehret, who had settled permanently in England after his visit to Holland in 1736. He enjoyed the patronage of some of the leading British plant collectors and of members of London's wealthy society. He was so sought after as a teacher by "the highest nobility in England", he wrote, that "If I could have divided myself into twenty parts, I could still have had my hands full."

Tab. XI.

LILIVM folis ſparſis,   *multiflorum, floribus reflexis,*
ſundo aureo, limbo auran-   *tio, punctis nigricantibus,*
   pedunculis ſingulis   *unico folio inſtructis.*

Bastard Jute, Blue Flag and Indian Chickweed

BASTARD JUTE, BLUE FLAG AND INDIAN CHICKWEED, *Ketmia Indica* etc., *Iris latifolia* etc. and *Alsine procumbens* etc. (now *Hibiscus cannabinus, Iris versicolor* and *Mollugo verticillata*). Hand coloured engraving after his own drawing by Georg Dionysius Ehret. Plate 6 from his *Plantae et papiliones rariores*, 1748–1762. Size of plate 21″ × 15″.

Plantae et papiliones rariores is unusual among Ehret's works in that it was an enterprise entirely his own. It may have been a desire to supplement his income that led him in 1748 to begin issuing a series of carefully hand-coloured plates that he had drawn, engraved and published himself. To ensure financial success, it was aimed at "the 'general world', who enjoyed looking at pictures of plants, with some botanical instruction included, if pleasantly presented".

The style of composition adopted by Ehret looks back to the late seventeenth century, when butterflies and plants were often depicted together. This plate bears a remarkable family likeness to the example of Nicolas Robert's work, published more than eighty years earlier, which is reproduced in the Introduction. Its elegant design could be termed "pretty", an inappropriately trivial adjective for most of Ehret's work. In choosing the subjects for illustration, Ehret was aware of the prevalent passion for "exotics", a term at that time applied mainly to newly introduced species that had rarely, if ever, been illustrated.

There is no obvious theme uniting an Indian *Hibiscus* (used as a source of fibre), a North American *Iris* and a tropical weed resembling, but not closely related to, chickweed. Typically, however, Ehret has arranged them in a pleasing integrated design. The vignette of *Hibiscus cannabinus* growing in a pot, which shows its habit, is characteristic of the plates in this work. The series of polynomials engraved on the plates are a reminder that Linnaeus had not yet published his *Species plantarum*, in which binomials were first used consistently.

Although Ehret wrote an autobiographical memoir, he did not say how and when he learned the art of engraving. The first known example of his use of the technique is his table showing the Linnaean Sexual System of Classification. His most important engraved work is in *Plantae et papiliones rariores* and *Plantae selectae* (engraved by Haid). All the engravings, however, constitute but a small proportion of his output; he left a large number of superb drawings which are rarely seen and of which regrettably few have been published.

Tab. VI.

1. KETMIA *Indica foliis digitatis flore magno sulphureo, umbone atro purpureo, pediculis foliorum spinosis.*
2. IRIS *latifolia Virginiana florum petalis repandis purpureis, erectis cœruleo variegatis. Miller.*
3. ALSINE *procumbens, Gallii facie Africana. 11.24.*

Imperial Gloriosa

IMPERIAL GLORIOSA, GLORY LILY, *Gloriosa superba* (double form). Hand coloured engraving. Plate 13 from John Hill's *Exotic Botany, illustrated in thirty five figures of Curious and Elegant Plants explaining the Sexual System and Tending to give some New Lights into the Vegetable Philosophy*, 1759. Size of plate 18½″ × 11½″.

The polymath Sir John Hill – apothecary, botanist, actor, gardener, landscape architect and journalist – was at heart a scientist. He admired Linnaeus, though not always uncritically, and one of his objects in producing *Exotic Botany* was to "illustrate the Sexual System" (of Linnaeus). Another was "to shew the course of nature in constructing double flowers".

The *Gloriosa* shown here obviously delighted him, for he had previously "been accustomed to receive this Species with single Flowers from the West Indies" and had not even heard of a double form. He considered it a plant of "vast Singularity and Elegance", qualities captured with great vigour in this unusual illustration.

It is clear from his text that Hill considered doubleness a highly desirable quality in a garden flower. Writing about tulips, he explained the processes by which doubleness occurs and gave advice on how to encourage the character. Of the *Gloriosa* he said, "the Doubleness is formed just as in the Tulip, but is not quite so perfect". He realised, however, that his specimen was not necessarily typical, for it had been found by a collector whose movements were limited by the travel restrictions then affecting Europeans in the Chinese Treaty Ports. He suggested that "in the Gardens of China doubtless a perfect *Gloriosa* might have been found: but the Gentleman who collected for me could not have the same Advantages as if he had undertaken the friendly task in Europe". The Chinese, he claimed, boasted that they had produced this double form by art, but Hill considered it a natural phenomenon.

The plates in *Exotic Botany* may well have been engraved after drawings by Hill himself, although they are not signed. In them the demands of botany complete with those of pure decoration. The drawings often had to be made from dried specimens, which Hill "brought to the state wherein they are represented in these designs, by maceration in warm water". To his regret, this process destroyed the specimens: "I could have wished to save some of these, but they were sacrificed to the work; and I hope their remembrance will live in the designs." His interest did not end there, for he took the opportunity afforded by his collections to conduct an extensive and well thought out horticultural experiment. "The seeds of these Plants came over with the specimens, and they are now in the ground, in four remote parts of the Kingdom . . . in all these places each Plant will be tried in the Stove, the Green-house and the open Air. This way we shall know what each will bear: and there is no other."

Pl.13

Imperial Gloriosa.

Tawhero

TAWHERO, *Weinmannia silvicola*. Engraving by Daniel Mackenzie after a finished drawing by James Miller (1775), based on an outline drawing by Sydney Parkinson (1770). Plate 436 from *Banks' Florilegium*. Printed in colour from the original copper plate, using contemporary techniques, and finished by hand. Alecto Historical Editions in association with the British Museum (Natural History), London, 1980–1990. Size of plate 28¾″ × 22¼″.

Sydney Parkinson made the sketches from which this *Weinmannia* and the *Dillenia* (Page 35) were drawn during the eventful course of one of the great voyages of discovery – Captain James Cook's first circumnavigation of the world. The expedition left Plymouth on HMS *Endeavour* in 1768 with instructions from the Royal Society to sail to the Pacific to observe the transit of Venus. Aboard was a small party of "scientific gentlemen" with their servants; they had been selected by the expedition's naturalist, Joseph Banks, then a young man of twenty-five and already a Fellow of the Royal Society. There were two artists; Alexander Buchan was to draw the landscapes and Sydney Parkinson, who had been drawing plants at Kew under Banks' patronage, was the botanical draughtsman. Following Buchan's death in Tahiti, which left Parkinson as the expedition's only professional artist, he was assisted by Banks' secretary Herman Spöring, who was also a botanist.

Having reached Tahiti by way of Tierra del Fuego and the Straits of Magellan, they observed, as instructed, the transit of the earth's shadow across the planet Venus. Cook then sailed the *Endeavour* southward to explore New Zealand, where no European had previously landed, although the Dutch explorer Abel Tasman had reported its existence over a hundred years earlier. The expedition established that the main part of New Zealand consisted of two large islands. They landed at several places and were able to converse with the Maoris through a Tahitian chieftain, Tapara, who had accompanied them. Banks and the Swedish botanist Daniel Solander succeeded in collecting over four hundred plant specimens, most of which belonged to previously unknown genera. Some, they were fascinated to note, resembled plants they had seen in Tierra del Fuego. *Weinmannia silvicola*, pictured here, was collected in early 1770 at Mercury Bay, east of present-day Auckland. It is a plant of very limited distribution, occurring in the wild only in the northern part of the North Island of New Zealand, where it is becoming scarcer.

All this time, Parkinson had been making sketches of plants and animals seen on the journey. He managed to complete drawings made in Tierra del Fuego and Tahiti; but when he died on the way home, in his mid-twenties, most of his work was still in the form of sketches. These were worked up by other artists after the expedition's return to England in July 1771. The sketch of *Weinmannia silvicola* was completed in 1775 by James Miller, a son of John Miller (see Pages 37 and 39).

Red Beech

RED BEECH, GOLDEN GUINEA TREE, *Dillenia alata*. Engraving by Gerard Sibelius after a drawing by Frederick Polydore Nodder (1778), based on an outline drawing by Sydney Parkinson (1770). Plate 1 from *Banks' Florilegium*. Printed in colour from the original copper plate, using contemporary techniques, and finished by hand. Alecto Historical Editions in association with the British Museum (Natural History), London, 1980–1990. Size of plate 28¾″ × 22¼″.

After leaving New Zealand, Captain Cook continued his circumnavigation of the world, sailing the *Endeavour* up the eastern coast of Australia. The expedition landed at a place so rich in plants completely new to the expedition's naturalists, Joseph Banks, Daniel Solander and Herman Spöring, that Cook named it Botany Bay. Later, Banks was to suggest the bay as a suitable site for a new penal colony. The early governors of the colony sent plants and seeds to him for the Royal Gardens at Kew, of which he was botanical director.

As the *Endeavour* sailed northward, an attempt to reach the open sea was thwarted by the Great Barrier Reef, where the ship was holed and the expedition nearly brought to a premature end. Fortunately they were able to reach a nearby river, which Cook named Endeavour and where they beached the ship, thus enabling the crew to carry out the extensive repairs that were necessary. The prolonged stay allowed the naturalists to make a detailed study of the surrounding area, one of their discoveries being the *Dillenia alata* specimen portrayed here. The red beech, a member of the ancient pantropical family *Dilleniaceae*, is the only species of *Dillenia* to occur in Australia, where it is found in the extreme north-east of Queensland; it is also native to coastal New Guinea. The bright yellow flowers, which last for only one day, earned this plant its Queensland name, Golden Guinea Tree.

Continuing towards the East Indies, Cook established that Australia and New Guinea were not joined together. Under his careful guidance the expedition's members had so far remained in good health, but in Java they were struck by malaria and dysentery. Both Parkinson and the assistant botanist Spöring died, as did several members of the crew.

When the expedition returned to England in 1771, Banks set about organising the completion of Parkinson's unfinished drawings, with a view to publishing an account of the botany in several volumes. He engaged Nodder, John Cleveley and the brothers James and John Frederick Miller to make hundreds of watercolours based on Parkinson's sketches, and he put in hand the engraving of the plates. Banks' librarian-botanist Daniel Solander, who had been with him on the *Endeavour*, was working on the text, but he died in 1782 without completing it. By then more than 700 copperplates had been engraved, but Banks never published either the plates or the text. Selections of uncoloured prints were published in 1900–1905 and 1973; but it was not until 1980–1990 that a complete coloured series of prints was produced, using Banks' engraved plates and contemporary techniques.

Dandelion

DANDELION, *Leontodon taraxacum* (now *Taraxacum officinale* agg.). Hand coloured engraving by William Kilburn from Vol. 1 of William Curtis's *Flora Londinensis*, 1777–1798. Size of plate 19½″ × 11½″.

The Dandelion is one of the most handsome of British weeds, one which has given pleasure to generations of children who have helped to disperse its fruit by puffing at "dandelion clocks". But, for all its attractions, there can be few gardeners who have not wished that its long taproot was less tenacious as they struggled to pull it up. If it were less common, and less successful in colonising places where it is unwelcome, the Dandelion would surely be a sought-after garden plant. Although its modern name is given above as *Taraxacum officinale*, the name applies only if most of the British and Irish dandelions are regarded as belonging to one species. Few botanists would accept this to be the case, but how many species should be recognised is a contentious matter, the study of which has become a specialist occupation.

Curtis noted that Dandelion was used for salads, particularly by the families of French descent in the Spitalfields district of London. They blanched it, "as the gardeners do endive . . . and it is remarkable that many plants containing bitter and acrid juices are rendered by this process mild, sweet and agreeable".

Flora Londinensis was an ambitious project conceived by William Curtis, the originator of the *Botanical Magazine*, who intended that it should at first include all the wild flowers growing within ten miles of London, which was then surrounded by fields and undrained marshland. If it had prospered, he had every intention of covering the rest of the British Isles. It was an ambitious project, extravagently conceived but inadequately financed; and for this and other reasons, Curtis ran into difficulties.

The plants were drawn life-size; but even the folio format did not allow every subject to be drawn complete. One plant that caused no trouble in this respect was the dandelion, which, like many of the plates in the first volume, was drawn by the Irish artist William Kilburn. Kilburn had been a calico-printer before his engagement by Curtis as artist and engraver; and after more than twenty years at work on the *Flora*, he returned to that more profitable occupation. According to Sir James Edward Smith, Kilburn used a camera obscura when drawing the plants.

After Kilburn's departure, Curtis employed James Sowerby and Sydenham Edwards to draw and engrave most of the plates. It is rarely possible, however, to discover the artist responsible for a given plate, as none were signed. Nor were most of them numbered, Curtis's original idea being that they could be bound finally in the order of the Linnaean System. The text, by Curtis himself, includes notes on the localities near London where he had seen each plant and, where appropriate, on its uses. *Flora Londinensis* is an important work; an idea of its influence can be gained from the fact that Sir Joseph Banks recommended it as a model for *Plants of the Coast of Coromandel* (Page 49).

Leontodon Taraxacum.

Blue Passion Flower

BLUE PASSION FLOWER, *Passiflora caerulea*. Hand coloured engraving by John Miller. P.74 from Vol. 2 of his *Illustratio systematis sexualis Linnaei – An Illustration of the Sexual System of the Genera plantarum of Linnaeus*, 1777. Size of plate 20½″ × 14″.

The name Passion Flower was given to this species by Spanish friars in South America, who were struck by the unusual form of the flower and saw in it a symbol of Christ's passion. Thus the three stigmas represent the three nails, two for the hands and one for the feet; the five anthers represent the five wounds; the corona represents the crown of thorns or the halo of glory; the five sepals and five petals stand for ten apostles (Peter and Judas being absent); and the hand-like leaves and whip-like tendrils represent the hands and scourges of Christ's persecutors. Passion Flowers come mainly from tropical America; and *Passiflora caerulea* is a native of southern Brazil, whence it was introduced into Britain in the seventeenth century. Unlike *Passiflora antioquiensis* (Page 119), which has long pendulous flowers, this Passion Flower does not need a pollinator that can hover. Its fruits have no edible value, but its fascinating flowers have long made it a favourite among ornamental climbing plants.

In 1736 Ehret had published the first illustrated table of Linnaeus's new system of classification, and it had been much reproduced and copied. As time went on, however, the need for a more detailed illustration of the system became evident; and it was in an attempt to satisfy that need that John Miller produced the historic work from which this plate is taken. It was issued in parts, beginning in 1770, and the eighty-five subscribers included Queen Charlotte, who was a student of both botany and flower painting.

Miller chose as his subjects plants which demonstrated the characters by which Linnaeus had defined the twenty-four Classes of his System. *Passiflora* illustrates his Class XX, *Gynandria*, in which the stamens and the ovary are united. Only plants of which living specimens were available were used, as Miller wished to show both the detail of the fruiting parts and the colour as accurately as possible, and he did not think this could be done satisfactorily from dried specimens. The consequent absence of representatives of "the more rare and curious Exotics" was a matter for apology. The first parts to appear were sent, through the Swedish Ambassador, to Linnaeus, who was effusive in his praise. He considered the work "more beautiful and more accurate than any that had been seen since the world began".

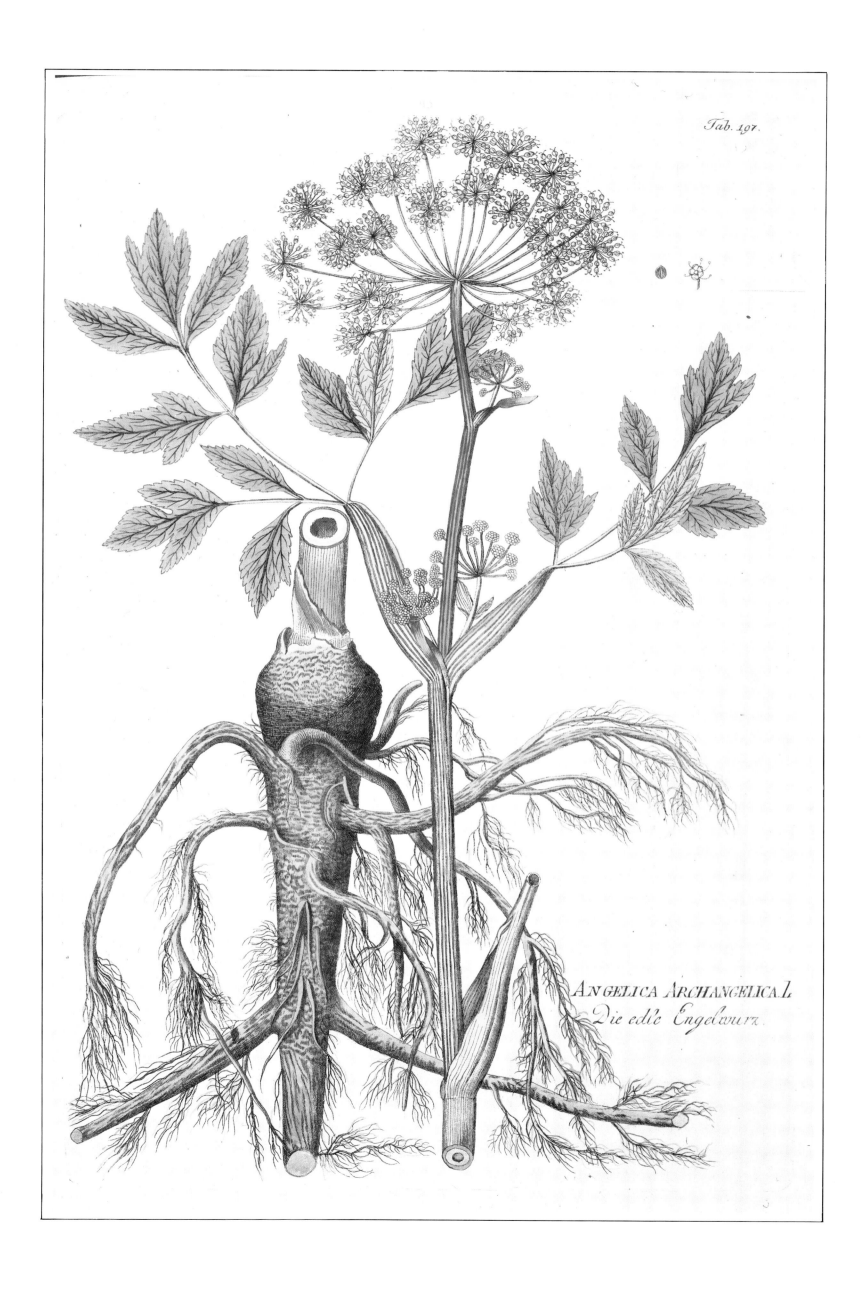

Tab. 197.

ANGELICA ARCHANGELICA L.
Die edle Engelwurz.

Roxburghia gloriosoides

Roxburghia gloriosoides (now *Stemona tuberosa*). Hand coloured engraving by Daniel Mackenzie after a drawing by an Indian artist. Plate 32 from Vol. 1 of William Roxburgh's *Plants of the Coast of Coromandel*, 1795–1820. Size of plate 22¾″ × 18″.

It seems a pity that application of the *International Code of Botanical Nomenclature* can prevent due honour being done to a worthy botanist. *Roxburghia*, a relative of the Yam family, was named in honour of William Roxburgh by Jonas Dryander – no doubt with the encouragement of his employer, Sir Joseph Banks. Unfortunately, the name *Roxburghia gloriosoides*, first published in *Plants of the Coast of Coromandel*, has had to be abandoned in favour of *Stemona tuberosa*, the name which had been given earlier to this species by the Portuguese Jesuit João de Loureiro.

Roxburgh was an Ayrshire Scot who started his career as surgeon's mate on one of the East India Company's ships and finished it as Director of the Company's botanic garden at Calcutta. An appointment as assistant surgeon in the East India Company's Madras establishment enabled him to spend much of his spare time studying the local plants with Johann Gerhard Koenig, a Dane who was at that time the Company's botanist in the region. This study of the Carnatic, an area between the Coromandel coast and the hills of the Eastern Ghats, was to stand him in good stead when, many years later, he wrote the work from which this plate is taken.

Following Koenig's death his successor, Patrick Russell, resolved to attempt a work on the useful plants of Coromandel, which he hoped would prove of real service to India. The Court of Directors of the Company sanctioned the publication, which Banks suggested should be modelled on *Flora Londinensis* (Page 41).

When Russell eventually returned to England, Roxburgh took his place and was thus able to devote more time to botany. He had made large plant collections in the Coromandel region and for some years had "retained a painter constantly employed in drawing plants". These Roxburgh had "accurately described and added such remarks on their uses" as he had "learned from experience or collected from the natives". At Russell's suggestion he sent the drawings and notes to the Court of Directors of the Company with a view to their being used for the projected publication, at the same time asking Banks to grant his protection to the work. Banks undertook to supervise the publication in London; he drew up a plan and an estimate of the expense involved, and with the approval of the Court of Directors the work went ahead. A selection of 300 drawings out of an eventual 2500 was published under the title *Plants of the Coast of Coromandel*, with text by Roxburgh and a Preface by Russell. Publication continued over a period of twenty-five years which almost coincided with Roxburgh's tenure of the post of Director of the Calcutta garden. The large plates of this lavish work were engraved in London after drawings by various Indian artists. The artists were accustomed to working in the very detailed manner which we associate with Moghul miniatures, and they had difficulty in satisfying the Europeans' demands for naturalistic representations. However, drawings such as this one of *Roxburghia gloriosoides* have a decorative appeal that compensates for any lack of realism.

To those who have been brought up on Edward Lear's *Nonsense Songs* the euphonious title of Roxburgh's work evokes at once memories of the Yonghy-Bonghy-Bo:

> On the coast of Coromandel
> Where the early pumpkins blow,
> In the middle of the woods
> Lived the Yonghy-Bonghy-Bo

Lear was a natural history artist of great distinction and must have known Roxburgh's book well. How pleasant to think that it probably triggered off this delightful flight of fancy.

Roxburghia gloriosoides.

Blue-eyed Arctotis

BLUE-EYED ARCTOTIS, WHITE ARCTOTIS, *Arctotis rosea* (now *Arctotis stoechadifolia*). Hand coloured engraving. Plate 162 from Vol. 2 of Nikolaus Joseph Jacquin's *Plantarum rariorum horti caesarei schoenbrunnensis descriptiones et icones*, 1797–1804. Size of plate 19″ × 13¼″.

Towards the end of the eighteenth century, when this *Arctotis* was growing in the Imperial Garden at Schönbrunn, the botanical exploration of its native South Africa was proceeded apace. Plants from South Africa had first reached Europe soon after Jan van Riebeek's original colonisation in 1652, and over the years visiting botanists had made studies of the area round the Cape of Good Hope. It was, however, primarily the work of four men, who ranged more widely and sent many plants and specimens to Europe, that sparked off the early nineteenth-century craze for growing South African plants.

The first of these collectors to arrive in South Africa was the Swede Carl Thunberg, in 1772; he was joined in the following year by Francis Masson, a Scot who had been sent out from Kew by Sir Joseph Banks. It was not until thirteen years later that the first collectors arrived from Vienna; they had been sent by Nikolaus von Jacquin to obtain plants for the Emperor Leopold II's garden at the palace of Schönbrunn. A severe frost in 1780 had resulted in many losses from the conservatories there, and it was decided to send expeditions to foreign countries to obtain new plants. Franz Boos and Georg Schall, two of the gardeners at Schönbrunn, arrived in Cape Town in 1786. After a year of collecting, Boos went on to Mauritius, but Schall stayed at the Cape for twelve years, sending frequent consignments of bulbs and seeds back to Schönbrunn.

It is not surprising, therefore, that Jacquin was able to include a very large number of South African plants in his magnificent florilegium. One of them was this charming *Arctotis stoechadifolia*, a fairly common plant of sandy places in the southern Cape. The individual illustrated here is not typical of the species, which usually has more yellowish "flowers"; the stems and leaves are densely covered with white hairs, which produce a silvery effect. Some idea of the enthusiasm evoked by these striking daisy-like plants may be gained from the fact that thirty-one species of *Arctotis* are included among the five hundred plates of Jacquin's *Plantarum rariorum*. In this, his greatest work on cultivated plants, he portrayed rare and exotic plants growing in the Imperial Garden, which under his direction had become one of the most celebrated gardens of its day. The drawings were made by a team of artists including Martin Sedelmayer, Johann Scharf and Franz von Scheidel.

T. 162.

Arctotis rosea.

Narrow-leaf Bottlebrush

NARROW-LEAF BOTTLEBRUSH, *Metrosideros linearis* (now *Callistemon linearis*). Hand coloured engraving. Plate 405 from Vol. 4 of Nikolaus Joseph Jacquin's *Plantarum rariorum horti caesarei schoenbrunnensis descriptiones et icones*, 1797–1804. Size of plate 19″ × 13¼″.

Callistemons, or Bottlebrushes, are confined in the wild to Australia and Tasmania. They belong to a section of the myrtle family which includes *Metrosideros* (from which they are now regarded as distinct), *Eucalyptus* and other genera. The fact that, at first glance, they look rather like some other Australian specialities, such as *Banksia* and *Grevillea*, is misleading. They are not closely related; but plants from the same area or habitat often exhibit a superficial resemblance to each other which does not stem from a true relationship. In many instances this resemblance can be attributed to adaptation to similar conditions. The name *Callistemon*, meaning "beautiful stamen", is appropriate for these eye-catching ornamental shrubs.

This *Callistemon* was growing in the Imperial Garden at the Palace of Schönbrunn, near Vienna, where plants from many parts of the world were in cultivation. Through its collectors, the Garden had particularly close connections with South Africa and the Caribbean; but interest in the flora of Australia was gradually developing, following the recent voyages of Captain Cook. A plant of *Callistemon linearis* had arrived at Kew in 1788, ten years before Nikolaus von Jacquin's sumptuous florilegium *Plantarum rariorum horti caesarei schoenbrunnensis* began to appear. In it Jacquin described and illustrated five hundred of the rare plants growing in the Imperial Garden, which, largely through his efforts and influence, had become one of the most celebrated in Europe. The first part of *Plantarum rariorum* is dated 1797, the year of Jacquin's seventieth birthday; soon after publication of the final part, when he was approaching his eightieth birthday, he was created a Baron. Through four reigns he had maintained a connection with the Imperial Garden that had begun when, after completing his medical studies, he had been sent by the Emperor Francis I to collect plants and animals in the West Indies. On his return he had combined supervision of the Garden with pursuance of his scientific work, and had become Professor of Botany and Chemistry and Director of the University Botanic Garden in Vienna. He was a competent botanical artist; notable among the works for which he provided his own illustrations is his *Flora Austriaca* (1773–1778), published in five impressive folio volumes, which is one of the major early European Floras. But in a busy life, during which he published several important works, he could not hope to produce all the illustrations himself; he did, however, find time to supervise the artists whom he employed, and under his expert guidance several artists of distinction developed their talents.

Metrosideros linearis.

Narrow-leaved Kalmia

NARROW-LEAVED KALMIA, SHEEP LAUREL, *Kalmia angustifolia*. Aquatint and stipple engraving by Caldwell after an oil painting by Philip Reinagle, printed in colour and finished by hand. Plate 28 from Robert John Thornton's *The Temple of Flora or Garden of the Botanist, Poet, Painter and Philosopher, being picturesque botanical plates of the choicest flowers of Europe, Asia, Africa and America*, 1799–1807. Size of plate 23″ × 18″.

The florilegium, which had been becoming gradually more elaborate during the eighteenth century, reached its apotheosis in Thornton's *Temple of Flora*. This splendid work was, however, only the third part of his ambitious botanical publication entitled *A New Illustration of the Sexual System of Carolus von Linnaeus*, presented as "a British Trophy in honour of Linnaeus". Thornton, who had qualified as a doctor of medicine, was a man of wide interests and published many books, mainly on botany and medicine. A substantial work on the *Philosophy of Medicine* had been followed by one on the *Philosophy of Politics*, and Thornton regarded his Linnaean work as constituting a *Philosophy of Botany*.

Despite all the emphasis on botany and Linnaeus, however, the scientific worth of *The Temple of Flora* is minimal; it is celebrated as a lavish and eccentric work of art. Thornton spared no expense in his quest for perfection, but long before publication was complete he was facing financial ruin. Everything about this work is sumptuous: the large folio size, the fine quality of the paper and the lavishly produced plates, which show the plants against a background of romantic, if not always appropriate, landscape. At times the emotional tenor of the text, with its flowery verses and patriotic tirades against Napoleon and the French, seems exaggerated. Indeed, the "British Trophy" was regarded by Thornton as part of a battle waged "in Finer Arts and Public Works" against "Gallia".

The artists commissioned by Thornton to make the twenty-eight oil paintings from which the plates were engraved were not all used to scientific work. Philip Reinagle, a pupil of the great portrait painter Alan Ramsay, is remembered for his animal and landscape paintings. He himself painted the landscape setting for the *Kalmia*, but some of the illustrations are the work of two artists.

Kalmia angustifolia is a native of eastern North America from Labrador to Georgia. It was introduced into British gardens in 1736 by Peter Collinson. Although it is a well known and charming garden plant, it can be dangerous in the wild, where it is highly poisonous to sheep – hence its name Sheep Laurel. In this beautiful print the *Kalmia* appears flooded with light as it stands against a dramatic background of lowering hills, poetically described in *The Temple of Flora*:

"High rise the cloud-capped hills where Kalmia glows with dazzling beauty, 'mid a waste of snows . . . "

The Blue Egyptian Waterlily

THE BLUE EGYPTIAN WATERLILY, THE BLUE LOTUS OF THE NILE, *Nymphaea caeruleá*. Aquatint by Stadler after an oil painting by Peter Henderson, printed in colour and finished by hand. Plate 32 from Robert John Thornton's *The Temple of Flora or Garden of the Botanist, Poet, Painter and Philosopher, being picturesque botanical plates of the choicest flowers of Europe, Asia, Africa and America,* 1799–1807. Size of plate 23″ × 18″.

Robert Thornton's grandiose scheme to produce a botanical book that would surpass anything published in France or elsewhere misfired in two respects: *The Temple of Flora* added little, if anything, to botanical knowledge and it was a financial disaster. In an attempt to finance his extravagant publication, Thornton indulged in publicity on a lavish scale. In fashionable Bond Street he opened "Dr Thornton's Linnean Gallery", where prospective subscribers could view the original paintings and buy a catalogue; but all attempts to raise sufficient funds failed, and publications of the *Temple of Flora* ultimately exhausted the considerable family fortune that Thornton had inherited when his mother and elder brother died within a short time of each other around 1797.

The Napoleonic Wars stirred intense feelings of patriotism in Britain at the time when the *Temple of Flora* was being produced, and Thornton no doubt hoped that these feelings would encourage many people to buy his highly chauvinistic work. Emotion is never far from the surface, often expressed in snippets of poetry:

> Shall Britain in the field
> Unconquered still, the better laurel lose? –
> In finer arts and public works shall they
> To Gallia yield?

Nelson's great victory over Napoleon's navy at Aboukir, near Alexandria, is related in detail by Thornton; and Henderson's portrait of the Blue Egyptian Waterlily shows it set against "a distant view of Aboukir and the waters of the Nile". Romantic imagination appears to have played its part in setting the "temple" against very European-looking hills.

The Blue Egyptian Waterlily is so named to distinguish it from the white waterlily that also occurs in Egypt (*Nymphaea lotus*). Both were well known to the Ancient Egyptians. The white waterlily was the Egyptian Lotus, so familiar as a decorative motif, while the blue was an object of veneration; the German botanist Schweinfurth identified petals of it in the funeral wreaths of Rameses II and Amenhotep I. Neither species, however, holds its leaves up above the water as shown in Henderson's illustration; this habit is characteristic of the true Lotus (*Nelumbo nucifera*), which is a plant of eastern Asia. Leaves of the Egyptian waterlilies normally float on the surface of the water. According to Thornton, the tuberous roots of this waterlily afforded a nutritious food to the Egyptians, who considered it to be an emblem of celestial love.

Erica speciosa

Erica speciosa. Hand coloured engraving by Henry Andrews. Plate 133 from Vol. 2 of his *Coloured engravings of Heaths*, 1802–1809. Size of plate 17″ × 10″.

It is easy to understand how the discovery of South African heaths, such as this brilliantly coloured *Erica speciosa*, sparked off a major horticultural fashion. *Erica speciosa*, which means "the showy heath", is one of the many fascinating ericas that arrived in England from the Cape around the turn of the eighteenth century, largely as a result of the collecting activities of Carl Thunberg and Francis Masson (see Page 67). Andrews wrote that it was almost impossible for the pencil of the artist to keep pace with the numerous importations from the Cape. He therefore resolved to illustrate first all the most elegant and desirable of the new arrivals. The atmosphere in which he was working must have been a stimulating one, for he talks of the "unabating ardour that still prevails in the science of botany, and rather increases than diminishes . . . " It is not surprising that he found "the limits of the genus impossible at present to prescribe", for there are over six hundred species of *Erica* and the majority occur in South Africa, particularly in the extreme south.

These showy flowers immediately attracted attention and their cultivation became the latest horticultural fashion. This soon developed into a minor craze so that, for example, one London nurseryman had five hundred species and varieties which, by careful selection, would provide bloom for every month of the year. It soon became apparent that Cape Heaths were not at all suited to the British climate. In Andrews' words: "The great difficulty attending the cultivation of many of the species . . . can only be surmounted by great care and attention to keep them from the partial damps and fogs so prevalent in this island . . . They should by no means be intermixed with other plants, but kept in a house entirely appropriated to them, and so arranged that the air may have as free an egress and regress as possible to them all." With such requirements, it was only to be expected that the craze would eventually die down, and by 1874 there were no more than fifty species in cultivation in England.

Andrews had access to the extensive collections of the Marquess of Blandford at White Knights, Reading, when making his drawings for *Coloured engravings of Heaths* and his other, five-volume work on this genus, *The Heathery, or a monograph of the genus Erica* (1804–1812). For these, as for his other publications, he drew, engraved and coloured the plates himself; and he also wrote many of the descriptions. According to Martyn Rix, the drawings were printed in green before being hand-coloured. The illustrations for *Coloured engravings of Heaths* are Andrews' finest artistic achievement, compared with which some of his other drawings look rather sketchy. They constitute a pictorial record of the genus remarkable for its content and for the consistently high standard of execution.

Erica speciosa, a native of mountains in the south-western Cape, was introduced into Britain in 1800. Its flowers are covered with a sticky "varnish", which adds to their lustre; but the effect is often marred by the bodies of numerous insects which become stuck to the surface.

Erica speciosa

Cedar of Lebanon

CEDAR OF LEBANON, *Pinus cedrus* (now *Cedrus libani*). Hand coloured engraving by Warner after a drawing by James Sowerby. Plate 37b from Vol. 1 of Aylmer Bourke Lambert's *A description of the genus Pinus*, 1803–1824. Size of plate 23¼" × 18½".

Lambert's *A description of the genus Pinus* is one of the earliest true monographs, and few if any of its successors can match its sumptuousness. The two large folio volumes contain accounts and full-page illustrations of most of the species then included in *Pinus* as well as other conifers and even some broad-leaved trees. The illustrations are mainly by Ferdinand Bauer, but work by his brother Francis, Georg Dionysius Ehret, Sydney Parkinson and James Sowerby is also included.

Sowerby's sole contribution to Volume I was this drawing of *Cedrus libani*, then regarded as a species of *Pinus*. This tree of Biblical fame was introduced into England between 1670 and 1680, when it was recorded by John Evelyn. Sowerby's drawing gives only a hint of the architectural qualities of the Cedar of Lebanon – one of the most magnificent and statuesque of trees. Few species can equal it as a specimen for a spacious lawn, where it is at its serene best framing a distant view. The details show long and short shoots, male and female cones, pollen and seeds.

James Sowerby was the founder of a family of artists and naturalists whose members illustrated botanical and conchological books for nearly a century. He studied at the Royal Academy Schools and soon developed an interest in flower painting which led to his meeting William Curtis, who gave him advice on botanical illustration. The two men became friends, collaborating on Curtis's *Flora Londinensis* and the first four volumes of his *Botanical Magazine*. Sowerby seems to have learned engraving largely by watching Curtis's engraver, Thomas Milton, at work. In 1791 Sowerby started issuing a publication of his own, *English Botany*, with text by Sir James Edward Smith. The heavy work entailed in making and probably engraving more than 2,500 drawings for this was no doubt the main reason for his collaboration with Curtis coming to an end, although until *English Botany* began to pay he had to support himself by teaching and painting portraits. Later, he published *Coloured figures of English Fungi* (1795–1803) and went on to study (and illustrate works on) zoology, mineralogy and fossil shells. In addition, after 1806 he engraved most of the plates for Sibthorp's *Flora Graeca* (Page 71).

When Sir Joseph Banks died in 1820, his mantle as host to the world's botanists fell on his friend Aylmer Bourke Lambert. Like Banks, Lambert formed an extensive herbarium and library to which he allowed men of science free access. According to *The Ladies' Magazine of Gardening*: "What Sir Joseph Banks's meetings were in his day, Mr Lambert's are at the present time; and every Saturday during the London season, his reception-rooms are crowded with persons eminent for their learning and talents, not only Englishmen, but foreigners."

While Banks was President of the Royal Society, Lambert was a founder member of the Linnean Society and became its President, and, like Banks, he was an ardent and experienced botanist. In between publication of his two volumes on the genus *Pinus*, he produced a monograph on the genus *Cinchona* (quinine).

Tab. XXXVII bis.

Pinus Cedrus

Black-seeded Kidney Bean

BLACK-SEEDED KIDNEY BEAN, EGYPTIAN KIDNEY BEAN, *Dolichos purpureus* (now *Lablab purpureus* subsp. *purpureus*). Hand coloured engraving by James Sowerby. Plate 74 from Vol. 2 of James Edward Smith's *Exotic Botany*, 1805. Size of plate 11¼″ × 9″.

The *Dolichos* which Sowerby drew for Smith's florilegium was growing in the hothouse of the Marquess of Blandford, whose notable collection of Ericas provided material for the drawings of Henry Andrews (Page 55). In the course of two years the hothouse had been completely overrun by the plant, which must have been a marvellous sight. Like the Runner Bean, this *Lablab* is a food plant which is so decorative that it is sometimes grown solely for its ornamental value. *Dolichos purpureus*, which is now classified in a separate genus, *Lablab*, is grown throughout the tropics for its beans. It is very variable, being divided into three subspecies, depending on the shape of the pods. The originally described form, flushed with purple in all its parts, was commonly cultivated in Europe in the early nineteenth century. Despite its common name, it is thought not to be a native of Egypt, only to have been cultivated there.

Plenck's *Icones plantarum medicinalium* (Page 43) may be considered a direct successor to the mediaeval herbal, with its concentration on useful plants. In the same way, the florilegium or flower book had continued to be produced in various manifestations throughout the eighteenth century, always including "rare and curious" plants. From his preface to *Exotic Botany*, it is clear that Sir James Edward Smith felt the need of such a work to publicise the exotic plants that continued to reach British gardens. He aimed to "introduce to the curious cultivator plants worthy of his acquisition from all parts of the globe, and to teach those who have correspondents abroad what to enquire for". This was to be done by illustrating both desirable new introductions and any earlier ones that had not previously been well drawn and published "in their native colours".

James Sowerby, who was engaged by Smith to illustrate the work, was able to make many of the drawings from living plants, but where these were not available there was no shortage of material. An insight into the atmosphere of co-operation that existed amongst a circle of enthusiasts for botany in those pioneering days is afforded by Smith's account of some of the sources on which he was able to draw. Aylmer Bourke Lambert (see Page 59) lent sketches made from Australian specimens, Captain Hardwicke offered the use of his collection of "accurate and beautiful Indian drawings", and Sir Joseph Banks had "freely offered, out of the abundance of his riches, any thing which may be desirable for this publication and for which he has no other particular destination".

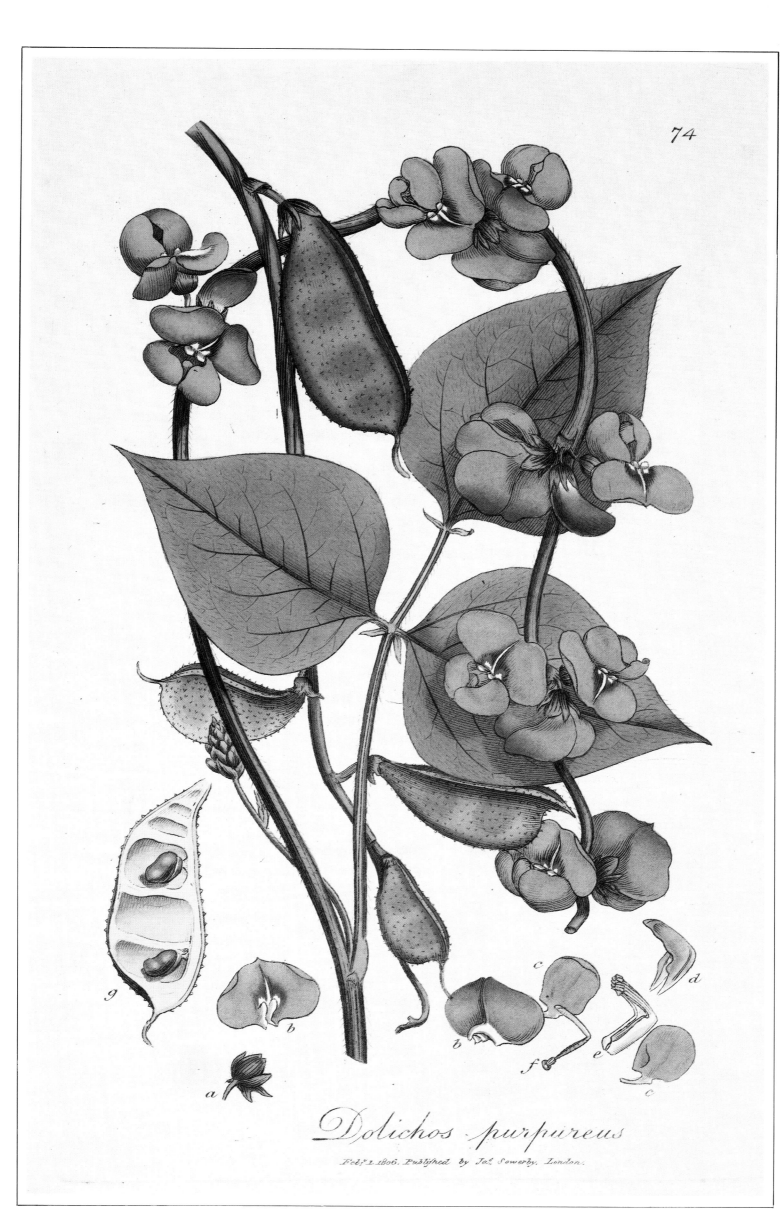

Dolichos purpureus

Feb. 1. 1806. Published by Jas. Sowerby, London.

Morocco Grape

MOROCCO GRAPE, *Vitis vinifera* cultivar. Aquatint printed in colour and finished by hand from a drawing by George Brookshaw. Plate 51 from his *Pomona Britannica: or, a Collection of the most esteemed Fruits at present cultivated in this Country; together with the blossoms and leaves of such as are necessary to distinguish the various sorts from each other. Selected principally from the Royal Gardens at Hampton Court and the remainder from the most celebrated Gardens around London.* Size of plate 22½″ × 18″.

Of the seventeen varieties of grape that Brookshaw considered worthy of inclusion in his book of "most esteemed fruits", he accorded this one a high rank. He wrote: "it may with some propriety be called the Emperor of Morocco, or King of the Black Grapes. This is a fine large handsome Grape, and cuts a noble appearance both in the house and in the dessert . . . nothing can present to the eye a more luxuriant view than a hot house well hung with a crop of them . . . There is a firmness in the flesh of this Grape, with a rich flavour which is pleasant, at the same time it is full of vinous juices." This was one of his subjects which did not come from the Royal Gardens at Hampton Court; it grew in the vine-house of Dr Lettsom, at Camberwell Grove.

Fruit has been grown in England with varying degrees of expertise at least since Roman times, and by the middle of the eighteenth century considerable advances in techniques of cultivation had been made. Thereafter, however, a decline in standards set in. In the Introduction to his *Pomona*, Brookshaw describes the sorry state of affairs to which fruit-cultivation had sunk: "there is scarcely one garden in fifty that is well planted. Many instances will be found, in some of the most celebrated gardens round London of long walls covered with trees whose fruit is not worth gathering; at the same time many of the best varieties have never been planted, but whether those inferior trees had been sent for others superior, or whether the fault was in the person who chose them, is uncertain; still there is ignorance some-where."

In an effort to dispel this ignorance, Brookshaw produced his *Pomona Britannica*, which "occupied nearly ten years' constant attention and labour". He dedicated his very large and splendid book to George, the Prince Regent, a fitting dedication for a work considered the finest ever published on the subject. Brookshaw emphasised the importance of planting the best possible variety of fruit tree and practising correct cultivation. His book provided a means of achieving the first of these objectives, but the second required experiments over a number of years to determine the best methods. He made his ideas clear: "there is every reason to suppose that grapes are not yet grown to that perfection they are capable of; but it should be the business of the Horticultural Society to try experiments to improve the growth of fruit. How much soever the subject has been neglected, it is of sufficient importance to demand attention." Evidently labour was more mobile at that time than one might have imagined, for he continued: "The short time gardeners are resident in any place, with their confined power, does not permit them to make experiments." The Horticultural Society and the Board of Agriculture took action to remedy the unsatisfactory state of affairs, and in the early decades of the nineteenth century set in motion extensive programmes of breeding and research to improve the standard of cultivation.

PLATE LI.

White Seed'd Rock

White Seed'd Rock, Cantaloupe Melon, *Cucumis melo* var. *cantaloupensis* cultivar. Aquatint printed in colour and finished by hand from a drawing by George Brookshaw. Plate 65 from his *Pomona Britannica*. Size of plate 22½" × 18".

Brookshaw illustrated nine varieties of melon and wrote that the Rock Melons were "in general allowed to be the best". The variety shown here was one of the best flavoured of his Rock Melons, distinguished from the others principally by its seed. All the melons are shown against a dark brown aquatint background, which gives them a distinctive air of luxury.

There is some doubt as to whether melons originated in Asia or in tropical Africa, but they have been cultivated for thousands of years, for example in Ancient Egypt. The Rock or Cantaloupe Melon was first grown in Europe from seed, at the Castle of Cantalupo in Italy, from which it gets its name.

Brookshaw aimed to illustrate all the best varieties of the different fruits, but tracking them down was not always easy. As he explained, "Melons are a great luxury to some, while others cannot bear them; in this work there are many varieties of them, all of which are extremely good sorts, but several of them are as little known, even by professional gardeners, as though they were not cultivated in this country. The difficulty I had to find out a gardener who could give me the information I wanted about two or three, was incredible; and if gardeners are so ignorant of them, how are gentlemen to know them unless they were delineated and a description as to their quality given?"

By making accurate drawings showing distinguishing characteristics, Brookshaw set out to provide his readers with the necessary means of making identifications. Ordering the desired variety from a nursery was no guarantee of obtaining it. He made this point by relating that "the same peach tree was frequently imported from France under different names; so that our nurseries . . . have been founded in error with regard to fruit trees, and no attempts have ever been made to correct them".

He dismissed the efforts of "every author who has written upon Horticulture and Gardening", saying that it was impossible to gain from their works the information necessary to plant a large garden with the best fruits. But at last help was at hand in the form of the *Pomona Britannica*. As Brookshaw put it, in his inimitable style, " . . . with the assistance of this book [gentlemen] will be as able to know what tree to have as any gardener or nurseryman" and " . . . by a little inquiry into the state of their gardens, may know if they have got those varieties of the different trees they wish to have . . . therefore this work would be ultimately a cheap purchase if it were twice the expense; and it must be considered, not as a work of utility for a short time only, for succeeding generations will find it equally necessary, useful, and advantageous; therefore it should be in every gentleman's library."

The highly idiosyncratic style of Brookshaw's Introduction to *Pomona Britannica* may seem to come close to hectoring, but his desire to bring about improvement shines out from the pages; every gentleman is to become his own expert. It is quite in keeping that, four years after the appearance of the *Pomona*, he published a book entitled *A New Treatise on Flower Painting; or Every Lady her own Drawing Master*. Blunt quotes him as having said, "Many ladies I have had the honour of teaching, sketched flowers so correctly after my manner, that I mistook them for my own drawings", and comments that "he had no higher praise to give".

Tassel Heath

Tᴀssᴇʟ Hᴇᴀᴛʜ, *Erica plukenetii*. Hand coloured engraving by Daniel Mackenzie after a drawing by Francis Andreas Bauer. Plate 9 from Bauer's
Delineations of exotick plants cultivated in the Royal Garden at Kew, 1796. Size of
plate 23½″ × 18½″.

The collection of thirty drawings of Cape Heaths, from which this plate is
taken, and *Strelitzia depicta* (Page 69) are the only major published works
of Francis Bauer, who is regarded by many knowledgeable critics as the
greatest of all botanical artists. Some disappointing lithographs after drawings by Bauer were published in Lindley's *Illustrations of orchidaceous plants*,
and he contributed in a small way to other publications, but the majority of
his exquisite drawings were never engraved and have therefore remained
largely unseen.

Delineations of exotick plants was produced in order to make known some
of the numerous plants that had arrived at Kew since the publication, seven
years earlier, of *Hortus kewensis*. South Africa had been a major source of
these, as a result of a particularly fruitful visit to the Cape by the Scottish
gardener Francis Masson. Over a period of twenty-five years he had
travelled widely on both sides of the Atlantic, collecting plants for the
Gardens at Kew. His collections of Cape Heaths had attracted particular
attention.

Many of Masson's latest introductions are illustrated in *Delineations of
exotick plants*, but *Erica plukenetii* had been known for some time. It is one of
the commoner Heaths of the south-western Cape, where it grows as a bush
up to two feet high on both the flats and the mountains northward and
eastward from Cape Town. Its proximity to Cape Town led to the early
discovery of the species; and a specimen reached Europe, where it was
named by Linnaeus after Leonard Plukenet, Queen's Botanist to Mary II and
Supervisor of the royal garden at Hampton Court, near London. This
illustration, meticulously engraved by Mackenzie, demonstrates Francis
Bauer's ability to convey texture and his great attention to detail.

Only fifty copies of *Delineations of exotick plants* were produced, and so it is
relatively rare today. It contains no text other than a dedication to Queen
Charlotte and an extended introduction by Sir Joseph Banks, in which he
points out that Bauer's drawings are so detailed that no accompanying
description is necessary: "It will appear singular at first sight, that engravings
of plants should be published without the addition of botanical descriptions
. . . but it is hoped, that every Botanist will agree . . . that it would have
been an useless task to have compiled, and a superfluous expense to have
printed, any kind of explanation concerning them." He goes on to refer
those requiring text to the forthcoming edition of *Hortus kewensis*.

Franz Andreas Bauer and his younger brother Ferdinand were born in
Feldsberg, Austria, but both worked for many years with great distinction in
England. Franz, who is better known by the English form of his name,
Francis, was prevailed upon by Sir Joseph Banks to settle at Kew, where he
lived and worked quietly for about fifty years. Under the generous
patronage of Banks he became Botanical Painter to George III and resident
draughtsman to the Royal Gardens at Kew.

Erica Plukenetiana?

Franc. Bauer del. Mackenzie sculp.

Bird-of-Paradise Flower

BIRD-OF-PARADISE FLOWER, *Strelitzia reginae*. Hand coloured lithograph by C.H. Bellenden Ker after a drawing by Francis Andreas Bauer. From Bauer's *Strelitzia depicta*, 1818. Size of plate 21½″ × 16″.

Queen Charlotte, consort to George III, was a keen and accomplished botanist. With her two daughters, the Princesses Augusta and Elizabeth, she received regular botanical instruction from the President of the Linnean Society, James Edward Smith; and the Queen and, for a time, Princess Elizabeth also took drawing lessons from Francis Bauer. Her patronage did much to make botany the fashionable subject it became in her day. It was very appropriate, therefore, that Sir Joseph Banks named one of the South African novelties at Kew after her: *Strelitzia*, because she came of the family of Mecklenburg-Strelitz; *reginae*, meaning "of the Queen".

The odd and fascinating inflorescences of Strelitzias are enclosed in a sheath, shaped rather like the bill of a heron, from which the flowers appear one at a time. These flowers are pollinated by sunbirds, in the case of *Strelitzia reginae* by *Nectarinia afra*. The birds alight on the perch-like sheath and, in obtaining nectar, deposit "foreign" pollen on the stigma, at the same time collecting more from the "arrow" for transfer to another flower.

Francis Bauer's paintings of various species and forms of *Strelitzia* were published without text. It was no doubt thought, as with his *Erica* illustrations, that they were self-explanatory, the details of the flowers being so clearly portrayed.

This clarity is typical of Bauer's work and bears witness to his deep knowledge of botany and skill with the microscope, as well as to the quality of his execution. The *Strelitzia* illustrations are so elaborately painted that they look more like originals than prints. The effect owes much to the lightness of Bellenden Ker's lithography, and it is interesting to compare the result with the more conventional engraving of *Erica plukenetii* (Page 29). *Strelitzia depicta* was one of the first books to use lithography, a medium which, for all its advantages, was a mixed blessing and made many enemies. Francis Bauer was, however, not among them and is recorded as having said, "I certainly prefer the lithographs, as for coloured plates they are much better than line engravings."

A sympathetic glimpse of Bauer in his old age is given by James Bateman in his book on the Orchids of Mexico and Guatemala. He describes Bauer as being well known to the botanical world as the *facile princeps* of microscopical draughtsman, and continues: "Although now between eighty and ninety years of age, he retains all his early fondness for his favourite science, and not unfrequently plies his pencil with no unsteady hand."

Sea Daffodil

SEA DAFFODIL, SEA LILY, *Pancratium maritimum*. Hand coloured engraving by James Sowerby from a drawing by Ferdinand Lukas Bauer. Plate 309 from Vol. 4 of John Sibthorp and James Edward Smith's *Flora Graeca*, 1806–1840. Size of plate 18½″ × 12¾″.

This exotic-looking member of the Daffodil Family is a common sight along the shores of the Mediterranean. Pancratiums must have had some special significance as long ago as the late Bronze Age; for when Spyridon Marinatos excavated the "Minoanized" town of Akrotiri on the island of Thera in the late 1960s, he found large and very striking frescoes of this plant on the walls of a room that seems to have been used as a shrine. Some experts now consider that the paintings are of Papyrus, depicted inaccurately on account of the artist's ignorance; but botanical evidence strongly supports their identification as Pancratiums. The flowers in the frescoes closely resemble Bauer's detail showing an opened-up floral tube. Akrotiri was abandoned around 1500 BC and was buried beneath volcanic deposits which marvellously preserved the *Pancratium* frescoes and others, some of which also depict plants.

Flora Graeca is generally accorded pride of place among illustrated floras; it is artistically superb and of broad scope and immense size, and its publication marked the culmination of an epic story. Its author, John Sibthorp, Professor of Botany at Oxford, arrived in Vienna in 1794 to study the great Dioscorides manuscript, the *Codex Vindobonensis*, before making an expedition to the eastern Mediterranean. His aim was to rediscover "the plants which were found in Greece from the most ancient times until the present day, and mentioned by the most capable writers, Homer, of course, Theophrastus, Dioscorides . . . " In Vienna, through the good offices of Nikolaus Jacquin, Sibthorp met the young and adventurous Ferdinand Bauer, who was persuaded to join him on his travels. They set off together in the spring of 1786.

Pancratium could well have been among the first plants they saw on their arrival in Crete, where they were "welcomed by Flora in her gayest attire". They spent June there, then, after sailing among the Greek islands to Smyrna, continued to Constantinople, where they remained during the winter. Accompanied by Sibthorp's friend John Hawkins, a classical scholar who was interested in botany, they sailed in the spring for Cyprus by way of Rhodes and southern Turkey. By the time they returned to Oxford, after spending the summer and autumn in Greece, the party had made specimens and drawings of more than two thousand plants.

Sibthorp and Hawkins made another journey to Greece in 1794, leaving Bauer in Oxford to work on his drawings; but Sibthorp returned with a fever that led to his death early in 1796 at the age of thirty-eight. His plans to publish the accumulated results of his journeys were explained in his will, in which he bequeathed his whole estate to the University of Oxford to be devoted to paying for the expenses. *Flora Graeca*, as the work was to be called, was to consist of ten folio volumes, each of 100 plates, along with a smaller unillustrated *Prodromus Florae Graecae*.

Sir James Edward Smith, President of the Linnean Society, was appointed editor of the *Flora* by Hawkins and his co-executors. Despite numerous other commitments and shortage of money, Smith persevered with the task, and at his death in 1828 six volumes had been published. Smith himself provided the descriptions of the plants, all of which were illustrated by Bauer's drawings. After Volume 7, edited partly by Smith and partly by Robert Brown, John Lindley took over as editor for Volumes 8–10, the last of which appeared in 1840, shortly before Hawkins died, having seen his executor's task completed. The other protagonist in this drama, Ferdinand Bauer, had long since returned to Vienna, and indeed had been dead for fourteen years.

Pancratium maritimum

Blue Pincushion

BLUE PINCUSHION, *Brunonia sericea* (now *Brunonia australis*). Engraving printed in colour and finished by hand after his own drawing by Ferdinand Lukas Bauer. Plate 10 from his *Illustrationes florae novae hollandiae*, 1806–1813. Size of plate 18½″ × 12″.

This delightful Blue Pincushion is the only known species of *Brunonia*, a genus named after its discoverer Robert Brown, naturalist on Flinders' expedition that circumnavigated Australia at the beginning of the nineteenth century. Brown was, successively, librarian to Sir Joseph Banks and first Keeper of Botany at the British Museum; he is known outside the field of botany for his discovery of protoplasmic streaming (Brownian movement).

The Blue Pincushion occurs wild on both sides of the Australian continent; the specimen that Ferdinand Bauer drew was collected on the coast of Queensland. It looks superficially like a scabious or even a blue thrift; but the conspicuous yellow pollen-cup at the end of the style betrays its relationship with the largely southern hemisphere *Goodenia* Family, in which it has often been included. What a pity that this highly desirable plant is too tender for our British gardens, where the range of true blue flowers is so limited.

Bauer and Brown were mutually congenial travelling companions, whose friendship was no doubt tempered by respect. Brown, a man of exacting standards, proclaimed that Bauer's drawings were, "for beauty, accuracy and completion of detail unequalled in this or any other country in Europe". The compatibility of the two companions must have been due in no small measure to Bauer's imperturbability in the face of danger or inconvenience. Only once, Wilfrid Blunt records, did he lose his temper – when water poured into his cabin, destroying some of his drawings.

Brunonia sericea.

Brown prod. fl. nov. holl. p. 590.

Madeira Foxglove

MADEIRA FOXGLOVE, *Digitalis sceptrum* (now *Isoplexis sceptrum*). Hand coloured engraving after his own drawing by Ferdinand Lukas Bauer. Plate 28 from John Lindley's *Digitalium Monographia*, 1821. Size of plate 18″ × 12½″.

After his return from Australia, Ferdinand Bauer did not confine his activities to his New Holland drawings (Pages 73 and 75). His meticulously drawn and artistically satisfying work appears in several publications of the time, notably in Lambert's *A description of the genus Pinus* (1803–1824), to which he was a major contributor. His illustrations of conifers for this pioneer monograph inspired Goethe to write: "It is a real joy to look at these plates, for Nature is visible, Art concealed." The brothers Francis and Ferdinand Bauer are pre-eminent among artists of whose work that remark could justifiably be made.

By the time that *Digitalium Monographia* was published in London, Ferdinand Bauer, who both drew and engraved this plate, had been back in Austria for seven years. It would appear that William Cattley, patron of the work, had been accumulating drawings of *Digitalis* for some time before he had an opportunity to organise their publication. In John Lindley, who had not yet begun his long career with the Horticultural Society, he found the person he needed for the task. Lindley wrote the descriptions and drew some of the illustrations, but plates by both Francis and Ferdinand Bauer are included.

William Cattley, a rich merchant and one of the most ardent collectors of rare plants of his time, was Lindley's first and liberal patron. He paid Lindley a regular salary to describe and illustrate new plants, and this fruitful partnership was responsible for both *Collectanea botanica* (Pages 89 and 91) and the work from which this *Digitalis sceptrum* is taken. Lindley acknowledged his generous support in dedicating *Digitalium Monographia* to "William Cattley – Patron second to none and best of Friends".

Digitalis sceptrum, which at first glance may not look much like a foxglove, is found only in Madeira. It is one of four foxgloves that are confined in the wild to the Atlantic Islands and are now regarded as sufficiently different from other foxgloves to be put into a separate genus, *Isoplexis*. Among their distinguishing characteristics are a woody stem and a stalked inflorescence. The plant portrayed here was collected in a shady wood in Madeira by Francis Masson; Bauer made his drawing from a specimen in Joseph Banks' herbarium. The copy of *Digitalium Monographia* from which this plate was taken was presented by Cattley to Ferdinand's brother, Francis.

Tab. 98

Digitalis
Sceptrum.

Tree Peony

TREE PEONY, MOUTAN, *Paeonia moutan* (now *Paeonia suffruticosa* cultivar). Engraving by Bouquet printed in colour and finished by hand, after a drawing by Pierre-Joseph Redouté. Plate 23 from Aimé Bonpland's *Description des plantes rares cultivées à Malmaison et à Navarre*, 1813. Size of plate 20½″ × 14″.

Josephine Bonaparte bought the estate of Malmaison in 1798 and soon appointed Redouté as her official botanical artist. She was determined to fill her garden with the rare and exotic plants that were pouring into Europe from all over the world, and in Redouté she found the ideal person to make a visual record of these riches. Years later, after her divorce, Josephine continued to live at Malmaison for a while; but it was too close to Paris for the comfort of Napoleon and his new Empress Marie-Louise, and so Josephine was given the chateau and estate of Navarre, near Evreux, together with an ample income. At first her "exile" depressed her, but as she involved herself in developing the garden at Navarre, she gradually became reconciled to the change. Redouté painted flowers in both of Josephine's gardens, but this peony was growing at Malmaison in earlier, happier days.

The specimen depicted here and another form of the Moutan had been growing in the garden at Malmaison for several years when Bonpland wrote his text; he was interested in the prospect for future cultivation in Europe of this luxuriant plant and noted with obvious pleasure that seeds produced by Moutans at Kew Gardens had been successfully germinated. The delicately coloured form *Paeonia suffruticosa* var. *banksii* was the first Moutan introduced into Britain; it was procured by one of the East India Company's "medical gentlemen" at the request of Sir Joseph Banks and arrived at Kew in 1787. The Malmaison plant would appear to be a similar form.

Peonies have been cultivated in China since the seventh century AD, when wild plants from the hills of northern China were taken to the Imperial gardens at Chang-an, where the ruling Tang dynasty had its capital. In the *Botanical Magazine* of 1809, Sims wrote that, although the Moutan had been cultivated in China for about fourteen hundred years, it was "considered in that ancient empire, according to the missionaries, as rather of modern introduction".

It is not difficult to see why tree peonies are so treasured; they have an exuberent beauty which is hard to resist and which Redouté has cleverly captured. How appropriate that the Chinese, on account of its Imperial associations and its sumptuous appearance, called the Moutan the King of Flowers.

Pæonia Moutan Thunb.

Orris

ORRIS, *Iris pallida*. Engraving by De Gouy, printed in colour and finished by hand, after a drawing by Pierre-Joseph Redouté. Plate 366 from Vol. 7 of his *Les Liliacées*, 1802–1816. Size of plate 20½″ × 13½″.

This beautiful Bearded Iris was an early introduction to the gardens of western Europe. It was thought to have come from Turkey, and this idea was still accepted in Redouté's time; but the species is now known to be a native of the mountains along the Adriatic coast of Yugoslavia and northern Italy, where it grows among limestone rocks. It was one of several species of *Iris* growing in John Gerard's London garden in 1596, and it undoubtedly played a part in the early development of the bearded irises that are such favourites of present-day gardeners. The many cultivars now available offer a wide range of rich and subtle colours, but *Iris pallida* is still worth growing for its cool elegance. Redouté has captured most beautifully the delicacy and silvery quality of its flowers, its leaves and its unique paper-white bracts.

Redouté worked for years to perfect his technique of producing colour-printed stipple engravings *à la poupée*, i.e. by applying the colours to a single plate with a rag-stump (*poupée*). This method promised a means of conveying, in a repeatable form, the luminosity and depth which he had achieved in his paintings on vellum. The technique was both difficult and expensive; indeed it has been described as probably the most complex reproduction method possible. When the colour-printing processes had been completed, the plates still needed to be touched up by hand. Redouté had a team of eighteen engravers working on the illustrations for *Les Liliacées*, which constitute his highest achievement in this field.

Producing illustrations by this means required generous patronage, and this became available to Redouté in 1798, when Napoleon's wife, the future Empress Josephine, appointed him her official artist to make a pictorial record of the plants in her new garden at Malmaison. With her patronage and friendship and an ample salary, he was able to embark upon the publication of his greatest works. Of these, *Les Liliacées*, which is dedicated to Josephine, is pre-eminent from a scientific point of view. It was an enormous undertaking, appearing in eight volumes over a period of fourteen years, and containing 486 plates, with text by three eminent botanists, Augustin Pyramus de Candolle, François Delaroche and Alire Raffeneau Delile. In a prospectus for the work Redouté wrote that the plants would be "drawn, engraved and coloured as true to nature as science may desire, and, what is even more difficult, with all the pictorial richness with which nature has adorned them".

Despite the name *Les Liliacées*, many of the plants portrayed (for example irises and crocuses) are not members of the Lily Family as it is now understood, though they are all petaloid monocotyledons. Both the choice and sequence appear somewhat haphazard, probably because Redouté drew his subjects as they came into flower and caught his eye. The resulting prints are of particular value as botanical records because some significant features of plants of this type do not show up well on dried herbarium specimens. Also of botanical importance is the fact that many species were either first named or first illustrated in the eight volumes of *Les Liliacées*, which provide an evocative glimpse of the wealth of "liliaceous" plants in the gardens available to Redouté.

Iris pallida.　　　　　　　　　　　　　*Iris pâle.*

P.J. Redouté pinx.　　　　　　　　　　　De Gouy sc.

Hudson's Rose

HUDSON'S ROSE, MARSH ROSE, *Rosa hudsoniana salicifolia* (now *Rosa palustris*). Engraving by Langlois, printed in colour and finished by hand, after a drawing by Pierre-Joseph Redouté. Plate (facing page 95) from Vol. 1 of his *Les Roses*, 1817–1824. Size of plate 21″ × 13½″.

One of the ambitions of Redouté's patron, Josephine Bonaparte, was to possess the greatest collection of roses in the world. At Malmaison she gathered together roses from far and wide and employed the best gardeners that could be found to tend them. Her garden provided Redouté with many of the subjects for his most famous work, *Les Roses*, which, like *Les Liliacées*, was an enormous undertaking. The first edition was published in thirty parts over a period of seven years, beginning in 1817, the year after the appearance of the final part of *Les Liliacées*. Redouté employed the same large team of engravers to produce the plates. Their quality bears out his statement in a prospectus for *Les Liliacées*: "Numerous experiments and a long search for the engraving method best suitable for colour printing, have shown me that art makes it possible to retain the magnificence and the manifold nuances which one admires in these flowers." *Les Roses* was an immediate success and has made him the best known of all flower painters; to many people his name is virtually synonymous with roses.

Les Roses has been described as Redouté's acknowledgement of Josephine's patronage of flower painting; it is sad that she did not live to see its publication. The text was written by Claude-Antoine Thory, a lawyer who devoted the latter years of his life to the classification of plants. The fact that the most frequently reproduced illustrations from *Les Roses* show cultivated, often double forms tends to obscure the comprehensive nature of the work. As Gisele de la Roche has written, "Redouté and Thory knew, described and figured almost all the important roses known in their day. Included were many of the key ancestors of our present-day roses. The plates in *Les Roses* have artistic, botanical and documentary value, both for the species and cultivars still surviving and for those that have disappeared."

This plate shows a North American rose, *Rosa hudsoniana salicifolia*, which Thory named in honour of "the celebrated English navigator Hudson who discovered the Bay which bears his name and where the rose grows naturally". *Rosa hudsoniana* is now included in *Rosa palustris*, which was introduced into Europe in 1726 from North America, where its natural range extends from Minnesota and Ontario eastward and south to Arkansas and Florida; it is closely related to *Rosa carolina*.

The delicate, comparatively small single flowers of this wild rose are strikingly different from those of the *Rosa centifolia* shown on Page 85, although the colour is similar. It is interesting to compare these two drawings, which show graphically the changes that have been achieved by hybridization and selection as rose breeders have attempted to satisfy horticultural taste. Tastes change, however, and many gardeners are rediscovering the delights of rose species and of the less highly evolved hybrids.

Rosa Hudsoniana Salicifolia.   *Rosier d'Hudson à feuilles de Saule.*

P. J. Redouté pinx.   Imprimerie de Rémond   Langlois sculp.

Provence Rose

PROVENCE ROSE, CABBAGE ROSE, *Rosa* x *centifolia*. Engraving by Langlois printed in colour and finished by hand, after a drawing by Pierre-Joseph Redouté from his *Choix des plus belles fleurs et des plus beaux fruits*, 1827–1833. Size of plate 12¼″ × 8¾″.

The form of *Rosa centifolia* portrayed by Redouté in this print is a triumph of the hybridiser's art; of its kind, it is surely near perfection. It is not surprising that *Centifolia* roses came to be identified with the so-called Queen of Roses cultivated by the Greeks and Romans. The notion is romantic, but informed opinion now believes it to be mistaken. *Rosa centifolia* is thought to be a complex hybrid of four species known in western Europe in the late sixteenth century, which was evolved over a period of about a hundred and thirty years and perfected in the early eighteenth century. The four species involved were *Rosa rubra* (the Apothecary's Rose or Rose of Provins), *Rosa phoenicea* (the Damask or Crusaders' Rose), *Rosa moschata* (the Musk Rose), and *Rosa canina* (the Dog Rose).

Early in the nineteenth century, Chinese species of rose, long cultivated in Chinese and Indian gardens, were first brought to Europe, which was soon in the grip of a rose-breeding fever. One of the most enthusiastic rose growers was the Empress Josephine, whose garden at Malmaison contained an outstanding collection of rare and exotic plants. Among her roses were many that Redouté drew for *Les Roses*, including several forms of *Rosa centifolia*, and it is likely that this one came from Malmaison. After her divorce from Napoleon in 1809 Josephine continued to build up her collection at Malmaison and, later, at Navarre; and until her death she supported Redouté with her patronage and friendship. Napoleon's second wife, the Empress Marie-Louise, was also his patron, and he had several pupils among the ladies of the court. Redouté never lacked wealthy patrons, many of them royal, and his paintings commanded high prices; but he lived on a more lavish scale than his income could sustain, and as he grew older he was increasingly plagued by financial worries.

Following Josephine's death in 1814, Redouté's income fell drastically and he had to borrow money which he had little chance of repaying. His great works, *Les Liliacées* and *Les Roses*, which had been made possible by Josephine's patronage, were primarily botanical, but necessity now forced him to turn to productions aimed at a wider market. The best known of these is *Choix des plus belles fleurs et des plus beaux fruits*, which consists of 144 plates depicting flowers and fruit painted by Redouté with the sole aim of achieving aesthetic effect. The resulting portraits may not be as satisfying botanically as those in *Les Liliacées*, but they are very decorative and abound in that particular charm which is the hallmark of Redouté's work. As William Stearn has remarked, Redouté "had risen to international fame by quietly producing pictures of plants, which by their freshness and their truthful rendering of beauty are of timeless appeal to all who love flowers as he did so wholeheartedly".

Rosa Centifolia.   *Rosier à cent feuilles.*

P. J. Redouté   Langlois.

Camellia japonica

JAPAN ROSE, Double White and Double Striped, *Camellia japonica*. Aquatint by Weddell after a drawing by Clara Maria Pope, printed in colour and finished by hand. Plate 5 from Samuel Curtis' *A monograph on the genus Camellia*, 1819. Size of plate 27″ × 21″.

Camellias must surely rank high in any list of choice garden plants. For sheer beauty of form they are hard to beat, and if they fall short of perfection it is, perhaps, only because most of them lack fragrance. As Curtis wrote, "they seem to strike the eye with dazzling perfection and we cannot but view with admiration the diversity and elegance of this beautiful family of plants".

Camellia japonica, the "Japan Rose", was first imported into Europe from China early in the eighteenth century. Although it is a native of Japan and Korea and has not been found wild in China, it has long been cultivated there as a garden plant. In Britain the wild species was introduced in 1739 and was later followed by cultivars, such as those shown here, from the gardens of Japan and China. Some of the first Camellias to reach Europe arrived by mistake in attempts to secure plants of tea, which is a species of the genus *Camellia*.

Curtis's *Monograph* is illustrated by five highly finished and dramatic folio plates by Clara Maria Pope. The text includes a list of "all the Camellias at present known . . . on the authority of Mr Lee of Hammersmith, a very distinguished cultivator of Exotic Plants". Details of each introduction are given, which show that the two cultivars portrayed here were "brought to England by Capt. Connor in 1792 for the garden of the late J. Slater Esq.". Lee's list occupies only a single page; but Camellias proved to be irresistable subjects for hybridists and propagators, and in the two hundred years since their introduction thousands of cultivars of *Camellia japonica* and other species have been produced.

Clara Maria Pope provided some of the most spectacular of botanical illustrations for Samuel Curtis's publications, which are now very rare. Those for his *Monograph on the genus camellia* and *The beauties of Flora* (1820) are certainly equalled, if not surpassed, by eleven sumptuous watercolour drawings illustrating species and varieties of the genus *Paeonia*. Curtis did not publish these, and they are now in The Natural History Museum, London. Samuel Curtis was a cousin of William Curtis, author of *Flora Londinensis* (Page 41) and founder of the *Botanical Magazine*, whose daughter Sarah he married in 1801. For many years after the death of his father-in-law, he was proprietor of the *Botanical Magazine*.

Although Clara Maria Pope spent most of her early life among artists, it was financial necessity that eventually led her to take up drawing, with a view to teaching. Her first husband, Francis Wheatley, painter and Royal Academician, was a man of unstable character whose extravagant and irregular habits had plunged him into debt; with four children to support, extra income was desperately needed. It was not until many years later, however, when she was around forty years old, that Clara Maria turned to the flower painting and botanical illustration which have made her famous and which caused Sir John Soane to comment, "this Lady's forte is particularly Flower Painting, in which she excels".

Cattleya labiata

Cattleya labiata. Engraving by C. Fox after a drawing by John Curtis, coloured by hand. Plate 33 from John Lindley's *Collectanea botanica*, 1821–1825. Size of plate 16½″ × 11¼″.

John Curtis's portrait of *Cattleya labiata* was taken "from a specimen which flowered in Mr Cattley's stove last November [1818]". It was "without exception . . . the handsomest species of the order that we have ever seen alive". Thus wrote John Lindley, who planned the publication of his *Collectanea botanica* when he was a young man of about twenty, helping Robert Brown in Banks' Library and Herbarium. It was to appear in monthly parts, illustrating "rare and exotic plants", and he was determined that "neither care nor cost should be spared in making it worthy of public support: . . . the price was only calculated to defray the actual expense of its publication". However, by 1821, when the first part was issued circumstances had forced him to "resolve upon abandoning the undertaking after the publication of four more numbers"; and so the enterprise came to a premature end in 1825. Forty coloured plates and one plain one had been published; most were by Lindley himself, though five other artists, including Ferdinand Bauer, John Curtis and William Hooker, contributed drawings.

Several of the plates are of orchids, a group of plants which particularly interested Lindley, and on which he became the leading authority. He named *Cattleya* after his patron William Cattley and expressed his pleasure at being able to pay this compliment "to a gentleman whose unrivalled successes in the cultivation [of orchids] have long since given him the strongest claims to such a distinction". *Cattleya labiata* was the first orchid to attract the envy of collectors. According to Lindley, it was found "by Swainson in the Brasils and sent by him to Dr W.J. Hooker" (see Page 93). Tradition has it that Cattley grew his plant from orchid material used as packaging by Swainson.

The artist John Curtis, like Lindley, came from Norfolk. In 1817 he went to London, where he met many of the leading biologists of the day, including Lindley. The following year he became resident artist to the *Botanical Magazine*, to which, over a period of thirteen years, he contributed more than four hundred plates. He does not seem to have been related to William Curtis, the magazine's famous founder. Entomology rather than botany, however, had long been his primary interest, and the work by which he is best known, *British Entomology*, was published in monthly parts during this same period. When failing eyesight forced him to give up descriptive biological work, he devoted himself to studying insects in a more practical way. His work in the field of pest control led to his being described as "a pioneer in a new epoch . . . one of the first professional scientists". Like the great garden designer Gertrude Jekyll, he became famous through a second career, forced upon him by the same adversity.

Tab. 25

Cattleya labiata.

J. Curtis del.   J. Swan Sc.

Catasetum hookeri

Catasetum hookeri. Hand coloured engraving by Weddell after a drawing by William Jackson Hooker. Plate 40 from John Lindley's *Collectanea botanica*, 1821–1825. Size of plate 16½" × 11¼".

This remarkable plant was collected in Brazil by William Swainson and sent to William Hooker at his home at Halesworth, Suffolk. Placed in the stove there, it flowered soon after its arrival, and Hooker made this drawing, which he sent to his friend John Lindley in London. This happened in 1818, the year in which the *Cattleya* shown on Page 91 flowered. Lindley published the *Cattleya* in 1821, but waited another four years before issuing the *Catasetum*. He explained that he "had long been hoping for an opportunity of examining this singular plant in a living state", but that, as far as he was aware, it had not blossomed again. He could therefore give "no description of it beyond that which might be obtained from the excellent representation now published". Appropriately, Lindley named the species after Hooker. It is one of the most striking species of a tropical American genus that includes some of the most unusual and handsome of all orchidaceous plants. Its flowering for Hooker, excellent botanist and plantsman though he was, would seem to have been achieved more by luck than good management.

At that time Hooker was living quietly with his family in Suffolk, where he had become a partner in a brewery; but the life did not satisfy him and he turned his thoughts towards using his botanical knowledge to improve his income. He asked Joseph Banks to let him know of any likely openings, and this led to a surprising change of career when, at the age of thirty-five he was appointed to the Professorship of Botany at Glasgow University. Although Hooker was well known as a botanist and had produced several beautifully illustrated books on the subject, as William Stearn has pointed out, "on paper he had no qualifications at all: he had never taught, lectured, or even heard a course of lectures". Banks, who knew his worth, had supported his application, and Hooker turned out to be an outstandingly successful professor.

The phase in his life that established him as one of the greatest figures in the history of British botany and horticulture began in 1841, when, after twenty years at Glasgow, he became the first Director of the newly nationalised Royal Gardens at Kew. Over the years, millions of visitors and generations of scientists have benefited from the fruits of his foresight and industry. Not only were the Gardens re-planned and the Museums of Economic Botany, the Herbarium and Library established, but building upon the tradition started by Banks collectors were sent out to obtain living plant material and herbarium specimens from many parts of the world. Throughout his twenty-four very busy years as Director, Hooker found time to indulge in a certain amount of botanical drawing, at which, as this illustration shows, he was more than proficient.

Catasetum Hookeri.

Thomsonia napalensis

Thomsonia napalensis (now *Amorphophallus napalensis*). Hand coloured lithograph by M. Gauci after a drawing by Vishnupersaud. Plate 99 from Vol. 1 of Nathaniel Wallich's *Plantae asiaticae rariores; or, descriptions and figures of a select number of unpublished East Indian plants*, 1830–1832. Size of plate 21″ × 14½″.

This handsome member of the Arum Family, like several of its relations, emits an extremely unpleasant smell, a characteristic which has deterred many gardeners from cultivating such striking plants as the Mediterranean Dragon Arum. Before its new leaf emerges in spring, *Thomsonia napalensis* produces an evil-smelling greenish-yellow warted flower spike surrounded, as is typical of the Arum Family, by a boat-shaped spathe, in this species up to eighteen inches long. A native of the central and eastern Himalayan and Khasi foothills, it is found in mountain forests up to 6000 feet above sea level. It was named in honour of Dr Anthony Todd Thomson, Professor of Materia Medica at London University – not, as might be expected, in honour of the Thomas Thomson whose name is so well known in Indian botany. *Thomsonia* was named many years before Thomas Thomson's collaboration with Joseph Hooker on the *Flora of British India*.

For years *Thomsonia napalensis* remained as the sole member of the genus *Thomsonia*, but it has recently been demonstrated that it cannot be kept apart from the large tropical genus *Amorphophallus*, which includes the gigantic Titan Arum. In this plant the inflorescence attains six feet or more, and its stench is much worse than that of *Thomsonia*. Despite this disadvantage, it was adopted as the official flower of the Bronx when it flowered in the New York Botanical Garden in 1937.

In India, where the old patronage had declined with the collapse of the Moghul empire, there were many artists who were glad to be given employment by Europeans. Early work on the Indian flora was done by "servants" of the Honourable East India Company, whose interest lay mainly in those plants which might be useful in "medicine, the arts or manufactures". Even though botanists often made their own sketches, they usually needed the services of botanical artists. Indian artists had been accustomed to working in a very laborious and precise manner, which was valuable in showing botanical detail, but their drawings had a stiff look to European eyes and lacked a feeling of organic growth. Several botanists trained Indian artists to work in a more "European" manner – Roxburgh has already been mentioned (Page 47) – and Wallich was one of the most successful. Cathcart sought artists trained by him at the East India Company's botanic garden in Calcutta to illustrate his Himalayan collections (Pages 117 and 119). One of the most accomplished of Wallich's protégés was Vishnupersaud, who drew several of the illustrations used in *Plantae asiaticae rariores*. The other artists whose drawings appear in this work are Miss Drake, Charles Curtis and Gorachand, another Indian trained at Calcutta by Wallich. The three hundred plates were lithographed by Gauci, who later worked on the superb illustrations for Bateman's giant orchid book (Plate 49), and were coloured by hand – often in surprisingly vivid hues. Their quality ensures that Wallich's book is a source of many visual delights and surprises.

Thomsonia napalensis

Bottlebrush Buckeye

BOTTLEBRUSH BUCKEYE, PAVIA DOUX, *Pavia edulis* (now *Aesculus parviflora*). Engraving by Bouquet after a drawing by Pierre-Antoine Poiteau, printed in colour and finished by hand. Plate 88 from Vol. 3 of Duhamel du Monceau's *Traité des arbres fruitiers*. New edition, augmented by Pierre-Antoine Poiteau and Pierre Jean François Turpin, 1835. Size of plate 21½″ × 14″.

Whoever heard of an edible Horse-chestnut? It is well known that the common Horse-chestnut has inedible seeds, in contrast to the Sweet Chestnut (*Castanea*) to which, despite sharing a common name, it is not related. Poiteau and Turpin, however, thought this one worth including in their monumental new edition of Duhamel's work on fruit trees. According to the authors this, the sole species of *Pavia* worth growing as a fruit tree, was discovered in 1792 by the celebrated explorer and botanist André Michaux "on the banks of the Savannah River, near the little town of Augusta, in Georgia". Evidently it was primarily valued as an ornamental, for we are told that, from material sent to France by Michaux, trees had been grown which, at the time of writing, were gracing the most beautiful gardens of the French Empire. In his drawing, Poiteau has subtly captured the fruiting *Pavia's* decorative qualities, but justification for its inclusion in the *Traité* lay in its edible seed. A tree was fruiting well in the orchard of the Museum d'Histoire Naturelle in Paris, and Poiteau and Turpin agreed with the head gardener there that the raw seeds had a tartness like those of other horse-chestnuts; they went so far as to caution people against putting them in their mouth. But when cooked the seeds were different; the verdict on the new "fruit" was that it could be added to the list of things which the rich man will eat to tickle his palate and the less well-off will find to be a nutritious and healthy food.

Whatever the merits of its seeds, the Bottlebrush Buckeye is a valuable small shrubby specimen tree for temperate gardens; it is easy to grow and flowers in late summer, when few shrubs are in flower. It was introduced into Britain in 1785, seven years before Michaux's discovery.

Poiteau and Turpin were members of the circle of botanists and artists who worked in Paris in the early years of the nineteenth century and collaborated with Pierre-Joseph Redouté in the production of superb hand-finished colour prints. Poiteau, who was originally a botanist, met Turpin in San Domingo, in the West Indies, where the latter was serving as a soldier. He inspired Turpin with an enthusiasm for natural history and the two men became lifelong friends. They worked together on some of the most important botanical publications of the time, forming an ideal combination: Poiteau the botanist who became a fine artist; Turpin the great artist who became a botanist.

Pavia doux.

Spanish Warden Pear

SPANISH WARDEN PEAR, BON-CHRÉTIEN D'ESPAGNE, *Pyrus communis* var. *culta* 'Bon-Chrétien'. Engraving by Bouquet after a drawing by Pierre Jean François Turpin, printed in colour and finished by hand. Plate 94 from Vol. 4 of Duhamel du Monceau's *Traité des arbres fruitiers*. New edition, augmented by Pierre-Antoine Poiteau and Pierre Jean François Turpin, 1835. Size of plate 21½″ × 14″.

This large pear's mouth-watering appearance is no misrepresentation; in the opinion of the authors it was not only one of the largest and most beautiful of all pears, but also sweet and juicy when fully mature and well grown. It is one of the old-fashioned Warden pears, named after Warden Abbey, Bedfordshire, where they were cultivated by the Cistercian monks. Characteristically, they are less given to rotting at the heart than many varieties, and this may account for their having been given the name Bon-Chrétien, which is thought to derive from the Greek *pan chresta*, meaning "all good". The Spanish Warden is a choice baking pear which was mentioned by John Parkinson in 1629.

Early in the nineteenth century, Paris was a focus of great activity in the field of botanical illustration. In particular, advances in methods of reproduction following the development of stipple engraving by van Spaëndonck and his brilliant protégé, Pierre-Joseph Redouté, had led to Paris becoming a centre of excellence in the art of botanical print-making. Among the many gifted artists who worked there was Pierre Jean François Turpin, described by Wilfrid Blunt as "possibly the greatest natural genius of all the French botanical painters of his day". Turpin learned the elements of drawing in the art school of his home town, Vire, in Normandy; but at the age of fourteen he joined the army and was eventually posted to the West Indies. It was a meeting there with Pierre-Antoine Poiteau that inspired him to devote himself to botanical painting; the two men became firm friends and were frequent and prolific collaborators.

In New York in 1801 Turpin met the German explorer and naturalist Baron Alexander von Humboldt, whose travels in northern South America and Mexico with the French botanist Aimé Bonpland have become legendary. The meeting led to the involvement of Turpin and Poiteau in the important botanical publications resulting from Humboldt and Bonpland's explorations. In these and other collaborative projects, Turpin was the dominant force. His work was always delicate and he excelled in detailed drawing of floral analyses. Later in life he turned these abilities to other botanical uses in studies of microscopic plants and plant organs.

Among Poiteau and Turpin's many joint projects, *Traité des arbres fruitiers* was one of the most splendid. It is a monument to the interest in fruit-growing that had been gathering momentum for several decades and had created a demand for another edition of Duhamel du Monceau's book, which had first appeared half a century earlier. The first edition had been of modest quarto size, with small uncoloured engravings, many taken from drawings by the great Claude Aubriet. A second, similar, edition had been published in 1782, but it could no longer satisfy demand. Poiteau and Turpin undertook production of a virtually new third edition, from which this plate is taken. It was much more imposing than Duhamel's original work. The six folio volumes are illustrated by 422 full-page engravings, 329 printed in colour and finished by hand. The variety of delicious-looking fruits in cultivation at the time is remarkable.

Bon-chrétien d'Espagne.

The Cannon Hall Muscat Grape

THE CANNON HALL MUSCAT GRAPE, *Vitis vinifera* 'Cannon Hall Muscat'. Hand coloured engraving by J. Clark after a drawing by Augusta Innes Withers. Plate 5 from Vol. 1 of the *Transactions of the Horticultural Society of London*, Second Series, 1835. Size of plate 11¼" × 8¾".

Augusta Innes Withers, Flower and Fruit Painter in Ordinary to Queen Adelaide and member of the Society of Lady Artists, was producing her exquisite drawings at a time when nice women did not sign their full name, but hid modestly behind the partial anonymity of a title. Her works are signed "Mrs. Withers", as those of her fellow contributor to the *Transactions of the Horticultural Society of London* and *Orchidaceae of Mexico and Guatemala* are signed merely "Miss Drake". The illustrations in both these publications are of exceptional quality. This is particularly remarkable in the case of the *Transactions*, which were primarily a vehicle for carrying out the direction of the Council of the Society that papers read at their meetings should be published.

The Horticultural Society of London was set up "for the Improvement of Horticulture in all its branches, ornamental as well as useful". A brief examination of the First Series of *Transactions* (1807–1830) reveals a wealth of interesting information, with an emphasis on the "useful" side. The Second Series (1835–48) began in much the same vein, but by the time the last volume had been reached the illustrations were predominantly of exotic ornamentals, such as the *Clianthus* shown on Page 107. The cultivation of fruit was a recurring topic, and the search for good new varieties is unending. When, in August 1831, a Mr Robert Buck sent the Society a beautiful and delicious white grape, the Assistant Secretary John Lindley recognised something special. He commissioned Mrs Withers to make this drawing and he prepared a paper to read to the Society's members.

The origin of the grape was unknown, but it had been given to Buck's former employer, Lord Bagot, by Charles Spencer Stanhope of Cannon Hall in Yorkshire. It was one of the finest and largest grapes in England, resembling the Muscat of Alexandria but ripening a full fortnight earlier when growing alongside it. Buck was growing his plant in a pine stove, for at this time pineapples were still being grown in Britain in heated greenhouses. The well-known fruit expert Robert Hogg considered the Muscat of Alexandria to be the parent of the more robust but less highly flavoured Cannon Hall Muscat.

As can be seen, Augusta Withers was an accomplished artist, and it is difficult to imagine that a print could be more realistic; for these grapes look juicy and ripe and just waiting to be plucked from the page.

Rosa rugosa

Rosa rugosa. Hand coloured lithograph by W. Siegrist after a drawing by S. Minsinger. Plate 28 from Vol. 1 of Philipp Franz von Siebold and Joseph Gerhard Zuccarini's *Flora Japonica*, 1835–1870. Size of plate 15″ × 11″.

The sweetly scented and robust *Rosa rugosa* is well known in western Europe, both in gardens and as a naturalised alien on sandy soils. In northern Japan it is found wild, particularly on coastal dunes and along sandy river banks. Von Siebold noted that the local people likened it to a pear on account of its large hips. However, he probably first saw it as a cultivated plant on the very small artificial island of Deshima near Nagasaki, to which the Dutch (the only foreigners permitted in Japan) had been confined since their arrival to found a trading settlement in the seventeenth century. Von Siebold reached Deshima in 1823 but soon escaped from its tiresome limitations. Because of his skills as an eye specialist he was allowed to visit Nagasaki, where he opened a school of clinical surgery. This unusual freedom enabled him to collect specimens and, in 1826, to help with what may be viewed as the first scientific survey of Japan. He remarked that the Japanese possessed a detailed knowledge of their wild and cultivated plants and that in Japan empirical botany had reached as high a level as in Europe. Although he was forced to leave Japan in 1830, when prohibited items were found in his luggage, he returned in 1859, after that country had been persuaded to abandon its traditional isolationist policy. His stay was brief, however, as in 1862 he retired to his native Bavaria to work on his extensive collections.

In China, where it is also native, *Rosa rugosa* was cultivated as long ago as the twelfth century, when ladies of the Sung court used its petals for *pot-pourri*. It became a popular garden plant in both China and Japan, and von Siebold saw many varieties of it in Japanese gardens, with pale red or white flowers and always single. In British gardens it is often found in double and semi-double forms, but looking at Minsinger's portrait it is easy to agree with those Japanese gardeners who preferred the perfection of the wild single form. This undemanding species pays liberal dividends to the gardener for minimal effort, and although it never produces the burst of bloom achieved by some roses, it scents the air with its sweetly fragrant flowers over a long period. The large handsome hips and robust foliage help to make it a useful hedge plant.

Tab. 28.

ROSA rugosa.

Maidenhair Tree

MAIDENHAIR TREE, *Salisburia adianthifolia* (now *Ginkgo biloba*). Hand coloured lithograph. Plate 136 from Vol. 2 of Philipp Franz von Siebold and Joseph Gerhard Zuccarini's *Flora Japonica*, 1835–1870. Size of plate 15″ × 11″.

Here we have one of the text-book Living Fossils, a survivor whose close relatives are known only as fossils. In evolutionary development *Ginkgo* fits in somewhere between the Sago Palms (Cycads) and the Conifers, but it differs widely from both. It is the only living representative of a group of plants, the Ginkgophyta, which was widespread in the Jurassic and Cretaceous periods. A member of this group, now extinct, was still growing in Europe during the Pliocene period, before the onset of the Pleistocene Ice Age.

A tall gaunt tree with fascinating leaves resembling those of the Maidenhair Fern (*Adiantum*), *Ginkgo* became a popular garden plant. Its leaves are variable to some extent, as the figure shows. Although trees are wholly male or wholly female, the males are usually grown in gardens, as the females have an unexpected disadvantage. In autumn, when the fruits are bruised as they hit the ground, their fleshy outer coat gives off an unpleasant odour, which for most gardeners outweighs any culinary merit that their kernels may possess. From them we get the rather weird name *Ginkgo*, which is derived from a Japanese name meaning Silver Apricot.

The *Ginkgo*'s survival has no doubt been helped by the fact that it has been cultivated in China, Manchuria and Korea from time immemorial, especially in the vicinity of Buddhist temples and Chinese palaces, where some specimens are reputed to be over a thousand years old. It was probably taken to Japan by Buddhist priests, and it was there that the German physician Engelbert Kaempfer saw it soon after his arrival in 1690 in the service of the Dutch East India Company. His account of his travels, *Amoenitates exoticae* (1712), includes the first European study of the Japanese flora and contains the earliest published description of the *Ginkgo*. His researches were made under the severe restrictions which confined foreigners to the tiny artificial island of Deshima – only 236 paces by 82 paces. These restrictions were still in force when the Swedish botanist Carl Thunberg arrived in 1775; but in three years, working under great difficulties, he studied the flora and collected several hundred specimens. His *Flora Japonica* was published in 1784 and was later complemented with illustrations based on his collections and on Kaempfer's drawings, which had been purchased by Sir Joseph Banks.

The third European to pioneer the study of Japanese natural history was Philipp Franz von Siebold, a Bavarian surgeon, who arrived forty-five years after Thunberg's departure and, like Kaempfer, was in the service of the Dutch East India Company. His *Flora Japonica*, a no-nonsense but generous book in which each plant has a full page illustration, is an example of the sort of international collaboration which characterises plant taxonomy to this day. This important work on the flora of Japan was written in French and Latin by two Bavarians (one of them of Italian descent) and was published in the Netherlands, where its second volume was seen through the press by a Dutchman; the drawings were made by German and Japanese artists and engraved by a German.

This unsigned drawing may well be, or be based upon, the work of Kuga Kuwahara, a Japanese artist who was taught by von Siebold to draw in the European manner, and some of whose work was included in *Flora Japonica* and in its companion publication, *Fauna Japonica*. In spite of the engraver's modelling, the predominant impression is of a two-dimensional pattern, which conveys a feeling of tranquility far more oriental than European and is particularly appropriate to the subject – a mysterious survivor from the ancient past.

Tab. 156.

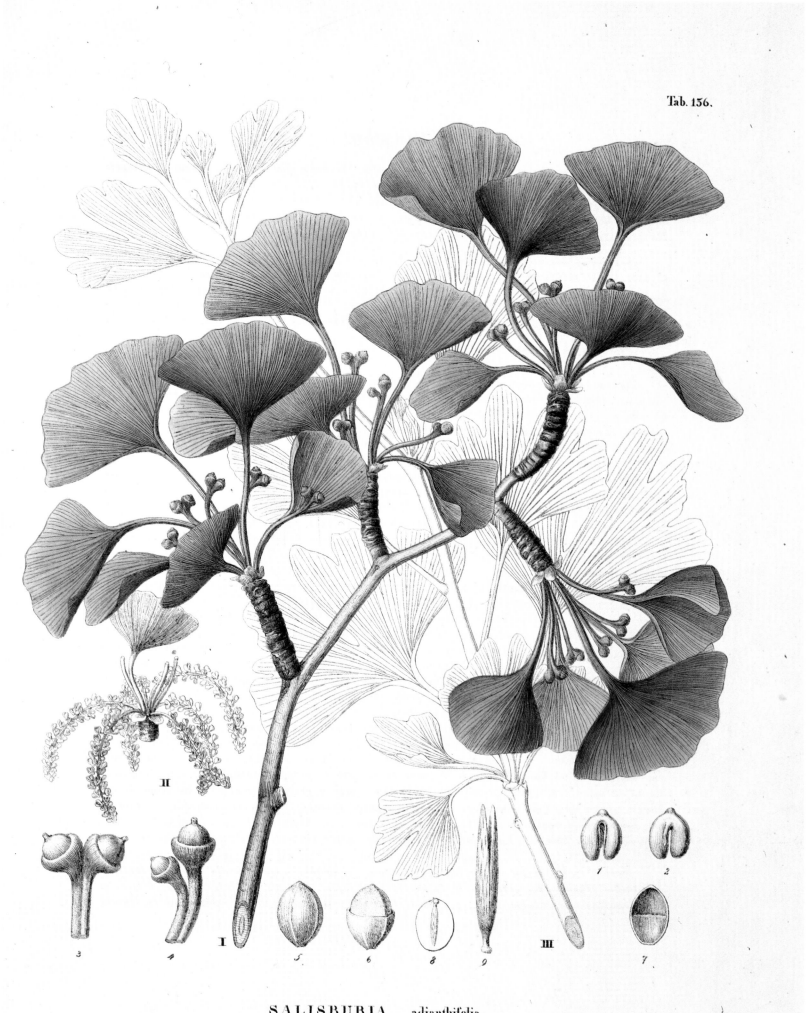

II

I

III

3   4   5   6   8   9   7

1   2

SALISBURIA   adianthifolia.

Bristly Rhododendron

BRISTLY RHODODENDRON, *Rhododendron barbatum*. Hand coloured lithograph by Walter Hood Fitch, based on a field sketch by Joseph Dalton Hooker. Plate 3 from Hooker's *The Rhododendrons of Sikkim-Himalaya*, 1849–1851. Size of plate 19¾″ × 14½″.

"One of the most beautiful of the Himalayan species" was how Joseph Hooker described this spectacular rhododendron. Although *Rhododendron barbatum* was already in cultivation in England, no coloured figure of it had been published before the appearance of this illustration, which, as Hooker remarked, would "serve to show what a treasure is in store for our open borders". He saw trees up to sixty feet high in the wild, but in cultivation *Rhododendron barbatum* is usually much smaller, forming a graceful tree with attractive smooth peeling bark. The bristly petioles which Hooker noted as a distinguishing characteristic show well on the drawing, and the painter has skilfully conveyed the rich glowing colour of the compact, globular head of flowers.

Publication of *The Rhododendrons of Sikkim-Himalaya*, at a time of growing interest in cultivating and hybridising rhododendrons, caused quite a sensation. Its author, Joseph Dalton Hooker, second son of Sir William Hooker, Director of the Royal Gardens at Kew, was already a scientist of repute. The Indian travels which yielded the material for the book were by no means the first that he had made in the cause of science. In his student days he had botanised in Ireland; and at the age of twenty-one, after completing his medical course in Glasgow, he joined Ross's expedition to the Antarctic. The resulting publications established Hooker's botanical reputation as a taxonomist and plant geographer. A period in England with the Geological Survey enabled him to pursue the study of British paleo-botany; but he was eager to make another botanical journey, and late in 1847 he set off for India. He arrived at Calcutta the following January, and during the next three years he botanised extensively in the area round Darjeeling, in the Sikkim and Nepal Himalaya and in the Khasi Hills of Assam. In the foothills Hooker found an abundance of rhododendrons whose splendour of colour could, in his opinion "only be compared with the *Butea frondosa* of the plains" (see Page 125).

Hooker sent the partially coloured sketches he had made in the field, together with seeds and dried specimens, to his father, who organised publication of the work and secured the services of the eminent botanical artist and lithographer Walter Hood Fitch. The sketches were scanty, and the fine illustrations that Fitch produced bear witness to his ability to make vivid drawings with the help of dried herbarium specimens. He is said to have had a marvellous power of visualising plants as they lived and of retaining their image in his memory. Joseph Hooker was delighted and wrote: "It has been one of my purest sources of gratification to find that the fruits of my own Himalayan journeys . . . have afforded to Mr Fitch the means of executing . . . a series of drawings that have been justly pronounced as of unrivalled excellence in an artistic point of view".

Tab. II.

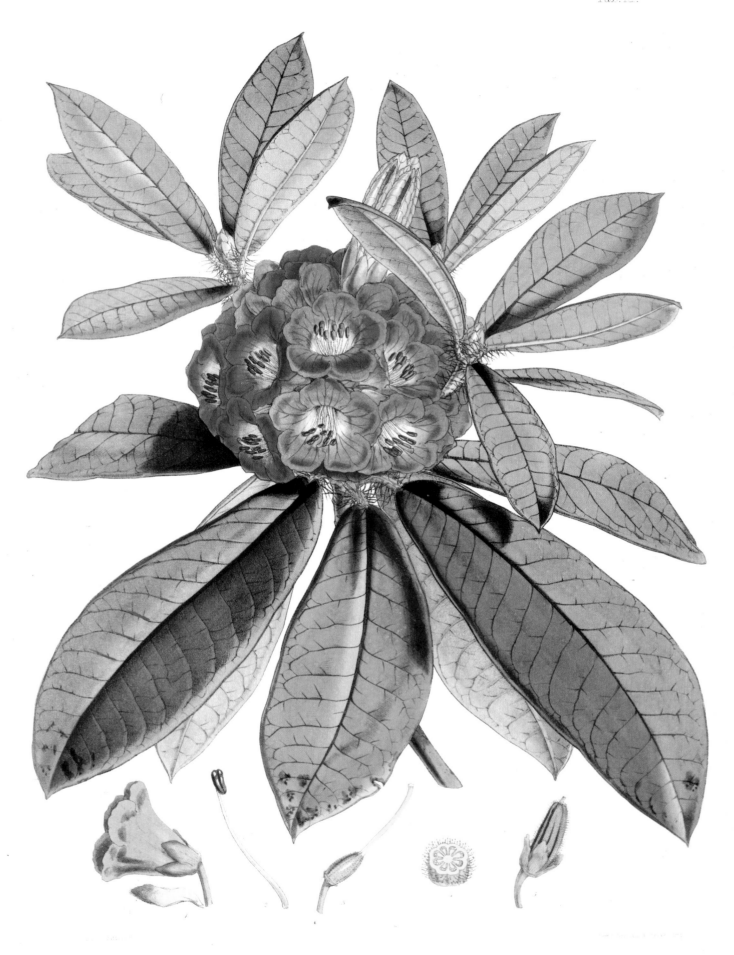

RHODODENDRON BARBATUM, Wall.

Major Madden's Rhododendron

MAJOR MADDEN'S RHODODENDRON, *Rhododendron maddenii*. Hand coloured lithograph by Walter Hood Fitch, based on a field sketch by Joseph Dalton Hooker. Plate 18 from Hooker's *The Rhododendrons of Sikkim-Himalaya*, 1849–1851. Size of plate 19¾" × 14½".

This exquisite rhododendron unfortunately proved too tender to grow in any but the mildest parts of Britain without the protection of a cool-house. Hooker found it in the inner ranges of the Sikkim Himalaya, growing in thickets to a heights of about eight feet, and noted that the foliage and flowers were faintly odorous. Of its name he explained: "I do myself the pleasure to name this truly superb plant in compliment to Major Madden of the Bengal Civil Service, a good and accomplished botanist, to whose learned memoirs on the plants of the temperate and tropical zones of Northwest Himalaya the reader may be referred for an excellent account of the vegetation of those regions".

The Rhododendrons of Sikkim-Himalaya was published in three parts, the last of which appeared in 1851, the year Joseph Hooker returned to England. His father, Sir William Hooker, had organised publication of the book and, as editor, had dedicated it to Her Royal Highness The Princess Mary of Cambridge, "whose taste for the pleasures of a garden, the first and purest pleasures of our race, has made her feel peculiar interest in The Great National Establishment at Kew". On his return to Kew, Joseph spent four years working on the collections he had made in India and on the information he had gathered there. In addition to the herbarium specimens, fruit and seeds which he obtained for Kew, he had amassed a wealth of information on the flora and vegetation of Sikkim. He had also collected fossil plants from the Gondwana deposits near Calcutta, and his survey work in Sikkim formed the basis of a map which proved to be of great value. He left an account of this very important expedition in his *Himalayan Journals* (1854).

From 1855 to 1865 Joseph Hooker was Assistant Director of Kew under his father; and soon after Sir William's death in 1865 he was appointed Director, a position he held for twenty years. As his biographer W.B. Turrill wrote in 1963: "It is perhaps not unfair to say that Sir William Hooker made the Royal Botanic Gardens as we find them today and Joseph Hooker made its botanical reputation by his own scientific contributions and by collaboration with, above all, George Bentham . . . He became the leading botanist of his age".

J. D. D. del. Fitch lith.

Reeve & Nichols, imp.

RHODODENDRON MADDENI, Hook. fil.

Talauma hodgsonii

Talauma hodgsonii. Hand coloured lithograph by Walter Hood Fitch based on a drawing made for James F. Cathcart by an Indian artist, with analyses by Joseph Dalton Hooker. Plate 6 from Hooker's *Illustrations of Himalayan Plants*, 1855. Size of plate 20″ × 14½″.

Although publication of a book of *Illustrations of Himalayan Plants* was inspired by Joseph Hooker's *The Rhododendrons of Sikkim-Himalaya* (Pages 113 and 115), it was not originally his own project. The idea came from James Cathcart, a Scot in the Indian Civil Service, who had amassed a large collection of botanical drawings by Indian artists and had resolved, upon the termination of his service in India, to "expend £1000 on illustrating a work similar to the Sikkim Himalaya Rhododendrons and to distribute it to the principal botanists and scientific establishments in Europe". He had first met Hooker in Darjeeling, and they met again in Calcutta in February 1851, when Hooker was on his way back to England, and Cathcart told him of the plan. They arranged that the drawings should be sent to Kew, where Hooker would keep them until Cathcart returned after spending some months on the Continent. Hooker went home to Kew and in due course the drawings arrived, but Cathcart had died suddenly in Lausanne in July 1851.

Hooker determined to publish the work himself, as a tribute to the memory of Cathcart. He made his selection from Cathcart's collection of drawings with the intention of conveying "some idea of the beauty and interest of that Flora to whose illustrations Mr Cathcart so zealously and liberally devoted his time and means".

Fitch's drawings for *The Rhododendrons of Sikkim-Himalaya* had been widely acclaimed, and Hooker now engaged him for the new book. He wrote: "I have been so fortunate as to secure the services of Mr Fitch, who has redrawn all the Plates, availing himself of my preserved specimens and analyses, and, by his own unrivalled skill in seizing the natural characters of plants, has corrected the stiffness and want of botanical knowledge displayed by the native artists who executed most of the originals."

The cost of publishing such a work was high. Hooker expressed an uncomfortably familiar sentiment when he wrote: "Science is not yet self-supporting; it requires the countenance of amateurs no less than the severe studies of proficients to ensure its progress." The long list of subscribers is headed by Queen Victoria and Prince Albert and includes Charles Darwin and the distinguished Swiss botanist Alphonse de Candolle.

Talauma hodgsonii was described by Hooker as 'exceedingly handsome', one of the noblest of the flowering trees of the Himalaya, surpassed only by *Magnolia campbellii*. He saw forests of *Talauma* in the valleys of Sikkim and also found it in the Khasi Hills of Assam. His attention was first directed to the trees when his guide excitedly pointed out "lilies and eggs . . . growing out of the ground". The "lilies" were fallen flowers of the highly scented *Rhododendron dalhousiae*, which was growing overhead in the canopy of oak; the "eggs" were the flowers of the *Talauma*, which drop before they open and release their spicy fragrance as they lie on the ground. Hooker named the species after his friend, the orientalist and diplomat Brian H. Hodgson, who had been his host for many months at Darjeeling.

Plate VI

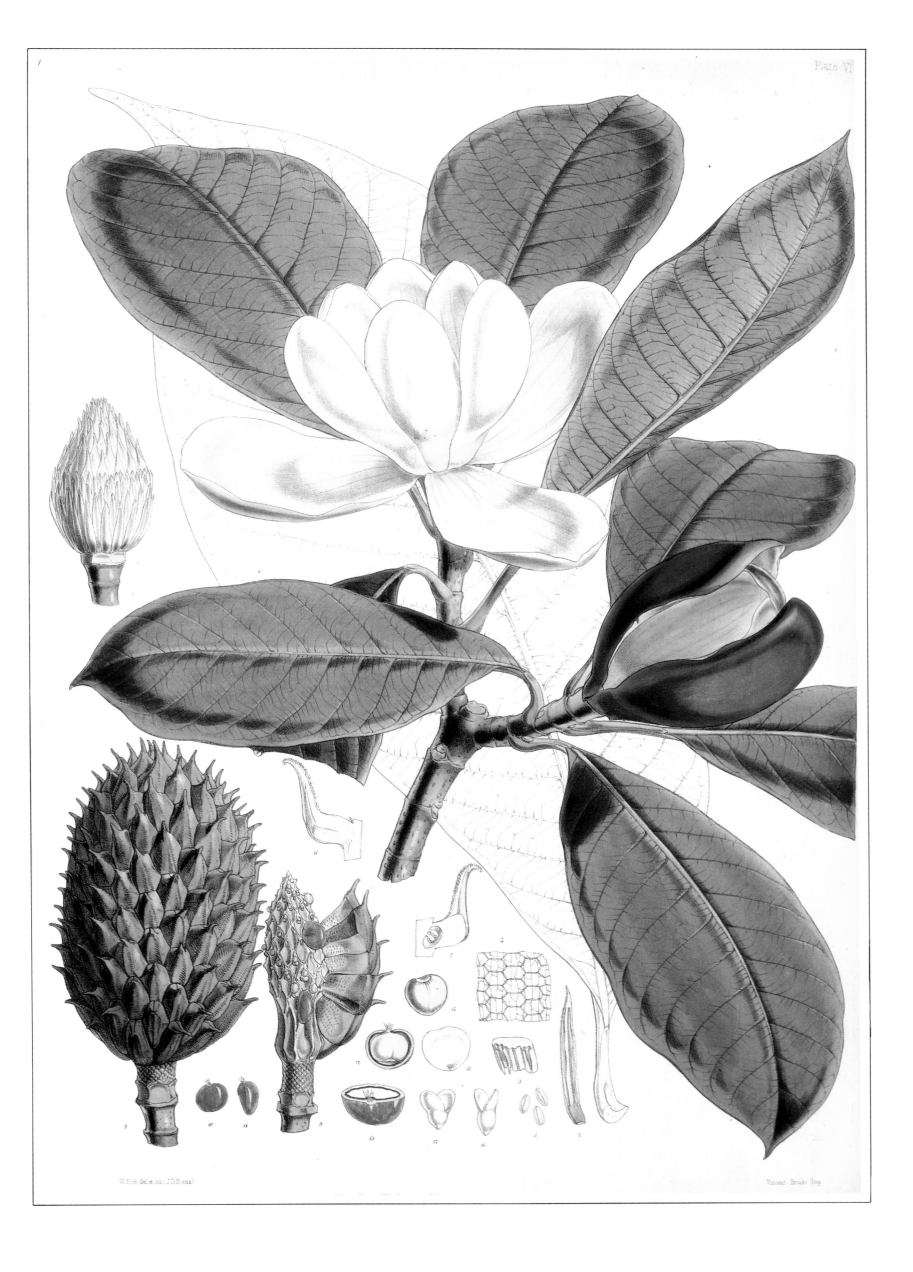

W. Fitch del. et lith. J.D.H. anal

Vincent Brooks Imp

Sikkim Larch

SIKKIM LARCH, *Larix griffithii* (now *Larix griffithiana*). Hand coloured lithograph by Walter Hood Fitch based on a drawing made for James F. Cathcart by an Indian artist, Plate 21 from Joseph Dalton Hooker's *Illustrations of Himalayan Plants*, 1855. Size of plate 20″ × 14½″.

"This very distinct and graceful Larch bears the name of its discoverer, Mr W. Griffith, one of the most active and promising of the many naturalists who have devoted their energies and sacrificed their lives to the pursuit of botany in India." Thus wrote Hooker of this elegant tree. Fitch's evocative vignette shows larches growing above a deep valley which draws the eye over distant foothills to the great snowy range of the Himalaya. The frontispiece to *The Rhododendrons of Sikkim-Himalaya* closely resembles this vignette and, according to Hooker, was inspired by the view from Darjeeling of "Kinchin-junga . . . the loftiest mountain yet known in the world".

Most of Fitch's lithographs for *Illustrations of Himalayan Plants* were based on drawings by Indian artists from the remarkable collection made by James Cathcart. Hooker's account of the origin of this collection provides a fascinating glimpse of a bygone world. Cathcart, youngest son of a Scottish judge, entered the Indian Civil Service and was posted to Calcutta. His health broke down more than once and, when his period of service was nearly at its end, he obtained permission to spend the last three months in the cooler air of Darjeeling. Hooker was in the area at the time and has described their first meeting, which occurred on a mountain track. Cathcart, who was on his way up to Darjeeling, told him that if the climate suited him, he intended to stay for a year or more and offered to help further Hooker's work by employing his artists in illustrating the botany of the area, which he knew Hooker was then exploring.

He lost no time in getting to work, for on returning to Darjeeling a few weeks later Hooker found "Mr Cathcart occupying a large house, surrounded by a broad verandah, from which baskets of orchids, etc. were suspended, and on the floor of which living plants of all kinds were piled in profusion. He had already established a corps of Lepcha collectors, who scoured the neighbouring forests . . . bringing every plant that was to be found in flower . . . and in his house were two artists busily at work . . . He intended to procure more artists . . . from Calcutta, especially those skilled ones who had been trained under Wallich and Griffith in the Botanic Garden, and to draw every plant of interest that he or I could procure". During the latter part of Cathcart's time at Darjeeling he kept as many as six artists steadily employed and accumulated a collection of nearly one thousand drawings of the hitherto little-known flora.

Hooker was indeed fortunate in securing Fitch's services in preparing the illustrations for publication, for to European eyes the Indian drawings often look rather stiff and lacking in botanical understanding. Fitch had been apprenticed to a firm of calico printers in Glasgow when he began to assist William J. Hooker (Joseph's father), then Professor of Botany, in mounting herbarium specimens. His aptitude for drawing soon manifested itself and Hooker repaid his apprenticeship fee so that Fitch could devote himself to botanical work. Under the influence of Hooker, himself no mean artist (see Page 93), Fitch's talent developed quickly; and when Sir William, as by then he was, became Director of the newly nationalised Kew Gardens in 1841, he took his young protégé south with him. Fitch was one of the leading botanical artists of his age and one of the most prolific of all time: nearly ten thousand published drawings by him were recorded in 1915.

Plate XXI

LARIX GRIFFITHII, HOOK.

Banana Passion Fruit

BANANA PASSION FRUIT, *Passiflora antioquiensis*. Hand coloured lithograph by Duwel. Plate 71 from Vol. 1 of Hermann Karsten's *Flora Columbiae*, 1858–1869. Size of plate 19½" × 13½".

The rose-red flowers of this exquisite Passion Flower have a narrow tubular base and hang, like lanterns, on remarkably long stalks – quite unlike the more familiar *Passiflora caerulea* (see Page 39). These features indicate that it is pollinated by hummingbirds, which are attracted by the reddish colour of the flower and hover beneath it to obtain the nectar accumulated at the base of the floral tube. Hummingbirds share with hawkmoths the ability to hover while reaching into long tubular flowers. Although *Passiflora antioquiensis* does not produce edible fruits, it is related to the granadillas (Passion Fruits). Duwel has skilfully conveyed the serene grace of his subject.

Passiflora antioquiensis was found by Karsten as a frequently cultivated ornamental in Bogotá, where it had been brought from the north-western Colombian province of Antioquía. The first published description of it was by Karsten, in the text accompanying this plate in his *Flora*.

Tropical South America, with its rainforest and strange plants and animals, had long attracted adventurous European naturalists. Maria Sybilla Merian had been an early visitor and had published the results of her work, which was primarily an entomological study (see Pages 15 and 17). Activities had, however, been limited by political and administrative constraints, and, even by Karsten's time, little had been published on the flora of Colombia. The distinguished Spanish physician and naturalist José Celestino Mutis, who spent forty years in Colombia in the late eighteenth century, had made an extensive record of the flora of the country, but it had not yet been published. More than six thousand drawings made by his team of draughtsmen were eventually sent with his collections to Spain, where they remained, neglected and unpublished, for a hundred and fifty years.

Such problems were not uncommon in colonial South America. Difficulties had curtailed publication of *Flora Peruvianae et Chilensis* by the French botanist Joseph Dombey, who had been allowed to carry out fieldwork only on condition that he was accompanied by two Spanish botanists, Hipolito Ruiz and José Pavon. Over a thousand drawings of plants in the neighbourhood of Rio de Janeiro, made for the Franciscan friar José Mariano Veloso, had fared little better. Several notable publications had, however, resulted from the biological and geographical work carried out at the turn of the eighteenth century in north-western South America (including Colombia) and Mexico by Alexander von Humboldt and Aimé Bonpland. Chance meetings and personal contacts can have far-reaching consequences. Humboldt's desire to travel had been awakened by a meeting with J.G.A. Forster, naturalist on Captain Cook's second voyage; and it was through a personal contact that he met the Spanish king Charles IV, who gave him permission to visit Spanish possessions in South America. Without his royal letter of recommendation, Humboldt's journeys and subsequent publications would no doubt have been very different. Karsten's involvement in tropical American botany, with which his name is especially associated, stemmed also from a personal contact, in his case a friend with business connections in Venezuela.

Passiflora Antioquiensis Krst.

Druck v. W. Horn in Berlin.

Scheelea regia

SCHEELEA REGIA (now *Scheelea butyracea*). Hand coloured lithograph by Duwel. Plate 176 from Vol. 2 of Hermann Karsten's *Flora Columbiae*, 1858–1869. Size of plate 19½" × 13½".

Hermann Karsten's first visit to the tropics, which strongly influenced his future career, was the result of an invitation from one of his friends, who had commercial interests in Venezuela. He was invited to stay at San Esteban, in a valley surrounded by the luxuriant vegetation of virgin forest. It must have been a revelation to a young man whose previous fieldwork had been concentrated in his native Prussia. He soon moved on to the German scientific and intellectual community of Colonia Tovar in the Andes. There he made his first study of tropical plants, on the palms of the region, which, together with tree ferns and cycads (sago palms), had particularly captured his imagination. It is not surprising, therefore, that his *Flora Columbiae*, which consists of descriptions and illustrations of a selection of the plants of the region, contains several drawings of palms.

In this plate, one can almost feel Karsten's enthusiasm emanating from Duwel's lively drawing. As well as portraying the sixty-foot high mature tree, with its feathery leaves, he has shown that the young leaves are entire and undivided. Like those of other palms, as they mature they begin to tear along the veins, and eventually each leaf separates into strips. Palms lack the strengthening round the margin that prevents this happening in most leaves. The Figures clearly illustrate the characters by which *Scheelea butyracea* differs from its closest relatives. Figures 1–9 refer to *Scheelea butyracea*, but Figures 10–11 and 12–15 show respectively fruits of *Scheelea excelsa* and *Scheelea macrocarpa*.

Such attention to detail is characteristic of all the plates in this work. Indeed, as the American botanist Alice Tryon has said, "The illustrations . . . are generally so accurate that the Karsten specimens are seldom referred to [for identification] in monographs including his species." It is not known whether Karsten's artists were familiar with the living plants, or whether their accuracy stemmed from botanical understanding and careful supervision by Karsten himself; but many botanical artists would be proud to receive such an accolade.

TAB.XXVI

Scheelea regia Karst.

Rose Apple

ROSE APPLE, *Jambosa domestica* (now *Eugenia jambosa*). Chromolithograph after a drawing by Berthe Hoola van Nooten from her *Fleurs, fruits et feuillages choisis de l'île de Java*, Third Edition, 1880. Size of plate 22″ × 15½″.

Berthe van Nooten was so struck by the beauty of the flowers of this curious-looking plant that she decided to devote a plate to it in her selection of choice flowers and fruits growing on the island of Java. There was a delightful bonus, too, for she wrote: "These pretty flowers are very ephemeral, as the corolla and the interior verticils very soon fall off – but in doing so they cover the ground as with a tapestry of roses".

This handsome small tree, which does not occur in the wild in Java, has long been cultivated in tropical countries for its flower, fruit and foliage. A related species, *Eugenia aromatica*, is the source of cloves. *Eugenia* was named in honour of Prince Eugene of Savoy, dedicated soldier and one-time ally of the great Duke of Marlborough.

The thirty plates in Berthe van Nooten's book are fine examples of chromolithography. The colour-printed images were overprinted with clear varnish, which gives a lustrous depth to the colour and has helped to produce illustrations of striking vivacity. The book was printed in Belgium, whose flourishing horticultural trade, like that of Holland, needed good coloured pictures of plants to attract sales. With a steady demand to support them, the lithographers and printers were able to develop their techniques to a high level. By no means all chromolithography was of such a high standard; indeed, the second half of the nineteenth century saw an increase in quantity going hand-in-hand with a decline in quality. In skilful and discerning hands, however, the medium can produce excellent results.

In 1876 the inveterate traveller and prolific painter of plants Marianne North visited Java and, in her own words, "made a pilgrimage to see the Dutch flower-painter, Madame von Nooten. She was very poor, and the Government had helped her to publish a large volume of prints, oddly and badly selected and not over-well done, but she was an interesting and most enthusiastic person . . . I bought a copy of her book and sent it home to Kew . . . but the ship was wrecked and it never reached its destination". However strange the selection may seem, the splendid plates scarcely merit Marianne North's rather sour criticism.

FLORES JAMBOSAE DOMESTICAE Rumph

Librairie C. Muquardt éditeur Bruxelles.

Bastard Teak

BASTARD TEAK, *Butea frondosa* (now *Butea monosperma*). Chromolithograph after a drawing by Berthe Hoola van Nooten from her *Fleurs, fruits et feuillages choisis de l'île de Java*, Third Edition, 1880. Size of plate 22″ × 15½″.

*B*utea frondosa was, in the opinion of Berthe van Nooten, "one of the most beautiful ornaments of the isle of Java and of the neighbouring islands". Joseph Hooker would probably have agreed with her, for he was clearly impressed by the splendour of its colour on the plains of India (see Page 113).

The tree from which this drawing was made was growing in the Botanic Gardens of Buitenzorg, in the uplands of Java; it must have been spectacular. The thinly set foliage of *Butea frondosa* exposes to view the numerous bunches of very bright flowers, hanging on panicles sometimes more than four feet in length. As Mrs van Nooten said, "one can easily imagine the striking effect of this tree in solitary and barren places, on the declivity of the mountains, where it is seen from a distance of several miles. Yet, so slightly do these flowers hold together, that they fall off at the least touch, and such is the brightness of their brilliant colouring that in strewing the ground they seem to deck the grass with coals of fire."

Berthe van Nooten was clearly an enthusiast where plants were concerned, but her personal life had become a struggle against adversity. One of the most remarkable features of her book is the profusely apologetic Preface, which makes sad, if fascinating, reading. She began by stating, "This work is particularly addressed to women. Its object, its tendency, its entire scope, all mark it with the special seal of our sex, whose mission and position are admirably described by one of the great writers of the present day, in those words at once so simple and so profound: 'Charity in humility'." She believed that in publishing a book she was guilty of committing an unwomanly act, for it was reprehensible for women to thrust themselves on to a stage which was rightly considered to be the provenance of men. She felt that she might be forgiven, particularly by women, if her predicament were understood. She explained, in highly emotional language, that death had snatched away the arm which was her sole support – the heart which was alone to be country, family and friends to her, leaving her in the spring-time of life, on a foreign shore . . . tearing away the veil of sweet illusions and placing her with a lacerated heart, a shrinking spirit and a feeble and suffering body before an unpitying necessity, which presented no other alternative than labour. With this came the derision of prejudice, which "plants so many thorns in the widow's and the orphan's path". The alternative to labour was privation, so she courageously set to work, producing a book which must have brought pleasure to many thousands of people who love flowers.

Peint d'après nature par M.me Berthe Hoola van Nooten à Batavia.

Chromolith. par P. Depannemaeker, à Ledeberg lez Gand. (Belgique).

BUTEA FRONDOSA. ROXB.

Librairie C. Muquardt, éditeur, Bruxelles.

INDEX